Everyday Enlightenment

Everyday Enlightenment

The Essential Guide to Finding Happiness in the Modern World

HIS HOLINESS

The Gyalwang Drukpa

with Kate Adams

RIVERHEAD BOOKS

a member of Penguin Group (USA) Inc.

New York

2012

RIVERHEAD BOOKS
Published by the Penguin Group
Penguin Group (USA) Inc., 375 Hudson Street, New York, New York 10014, USA •
Penguin Group (Canada), 90 Eglinton Avenue East, Suite 700, Toronto, Ontario M4P 2Y3,
Canada (a division of Pearson Penguin Canada Inc.) • Penguin Books Ltd, 80 Strand,
London WC2R 0RL, England • Penguin Ireland, 25 St Stephen's Green, Dublin 2, Ireland
(a division of Penguin Books Ltd) • Penguin Group (Australia), 250 Camberwell Road,
Camberwell, Victoria 3124, Australia (a division of Pearson Australia Group Pty Ltd) •
Penguin Books India Pvt Ltd, 11 Community Centre, Panchsheel Park, New Delhi–110 017,
India • Penguin Group (NZ), 67 Apollo Drive, Rosedale, North Shore 0632,
New Zealand (a division of Pearson New Zealand Ltd) • Penguin Books
(South Africa) (Pty) Ltd, 24 Sturdee Avenue, Rosebank,
Johannesburg 2196, South Africa

Penguin Books Ltd, Registered Offices: 80 Strand, London WC2R 0RL, England

ISBN 978-1-59448-623-4

Printed in the United States of America
1   3   5   7   9   10   8   6   4   2

Book design by Michelle McMillian

*Penguin is committed to publishing works of quality and integrity.
In that spirit, we are proud to offer this book to our readers;
however, the story, the experiences, and the words
are the author's alone.*

ALWAYS LEARNING   PEARSON

Contents

Part Three. Overcoming Obstacles Along Your Way

Everyday
Enlightenment

Welcome

A pilgrimage to travel to holy sites is traditional among believers of various spiritual traditions. Christian pilgrims go to Bethlehem, Jews go to Jerusalem, Muslims to Mecca, and we Buddhists walk on the world's rooftop, the Himalayas, to the various sites blessed by the presence of the Buddha and the generations of enlightened masters after him.

I love to walk during these pilgrimages. Once in a while, I arrange *pad yatra*, meaning "foot journeys" or walking meditations, for my students and friends. On these foot journeys, we spend a few weeks walking through mountains and valleys together. Often, we pick up plastic bottles and other garbage along the way and visit remote villages that rarely get to see outsiders.

These are journeys from *self* to *selflessness*. We are able to observe life at a gradual pace and realize the beauty in simplicity, in having enough food to keep us going and shelter over our heads at night. We accept whatever comes our way. We know that we are a part of nature, we *are* nature. Instead of pressing on the accelerator and absentmindedly rushing through the details of life, we can look around at the way others live, the way people interact and the way the sun rises and sets. In the end, it is just me and my consciousness, looking at each other, without fabrication.

It is my hope that we may walk together for a little while along your own uncommon path. Perhaps you will join, in your own life, what I jokingly call the Turtle Club. I started this group for my friends and students who could not walk as fast as their own groups while on *pad yatra*. And over time I have realized how good it is to be in the Turtle Club, how, really, I'd like to be their chairman!

I love the modern world; we have so many opportunities to be generous and inspire each other. But in the day to day it is easy to rush without paying much attention or taking the time to appreciate just how precious our life is. Our minds become wild and restless. We run toward some future hope or dream, or away from things in our past. We lose our connection with life, with ourselves, and forget to enjoy the journey. Or we begin to lose faith in the world around us; there are so many problems to think about, we put our blinders on and stop seeing what is right there, on the doorstep, what we can do to make a difference. We become attached to our rigid view of life, how we like things to be. But when the world doesn't fit in with our wishes and desires, we become frustrated and stubborn, we forget how to bend and be flexible, and life becomes difficult.

I feel that we should sometimes take a break from the fast track and slow down to look around us. This is why I like to often think of the Turtle Club. When we slow things down, it turns out we have *more* time to do the things that really matter, we can look around and appreciate all the details, we feel connected with our own body, our own mind, with all the people in our life, and with the world around us. Because *everything* in this life is connected; it's a case of how we *see* and appreciate those connections, how we cherish them. And to do that, we need to learn how to take things a little easier and take in the scenery of life. It's easier to walk with others at a relaxed pace, and often we have better stamina in the long run. We can chat along the way, noticing what catches our attention and really inspires us, and we have time to inspire others too. Right now this gentle, middle path doesn't often get the best press; it is a competitive world with pressure to be *the* best, when really life is about doing *your* best, today, because that is when it really counts.

Reading this book is your opportunity to take a break from the fast track of life and have a look around, to further your understanding, connect with yourself and then with others. You may begin to discover or get to know more deeply your inner cause and what you truly want to achieve. In essence, this is a gentle reminder to live your life with compassion, to be kind to yourself so that you may be kind to others. It will help calm your wandering mind and let go of your own and others' judgments and comparisons.

When we slow down to let go of judgments, we can truly observe the world and develop understanding of it. It is *understanding* that is the essence of all that is good in our lives and in the world around us. When we begin to look at others with understanding, we can put ourselves in their shoes, see things from their point of view and know that we are all in the same boat. Then a great sense of freedom opens up. Right now so many people live in fear or with an underlying anxiety. We live in a world in which the idea of control is very important; either we are under the control of others or we want to be the ones in control all of the time; it is a constant battle that never brings freedom or happiness, but rather expectations and disappointments. Husbands are in control of wives; wives are in control of husbands. Parents control their children, and now, more often, children control parents. We have forgotten how to be free and to be ourselves; or as soon as we are by ourselves, we feel lonely or sad—we have to look ourselves in the face and worry about what we might see.

The highlight of my own life is my *acceptance*. It allows me to enjoy every minute, whatever circumstances I am in, whatever my challenges and difficulties. It helps me to put judgments and comparisons aside; it helps me to know that I am good enough so long as I simply try my best in this life. It is this feeling of peace that I hope I can in some way pass on to you through the words in this book, or through my teachings and my movements, such as Live to Love. You don't have to be perfect, and neither do you have to lay that pressure on the shoulders of others. This understanding that we are perfectly OK, just as we are, makes us fearless, so that we may let go of all the nonsense and live our lives, making the world a better place, which is the best way to bring happiness into our hearts.

Steps Along the Way

Each of us has a path, and to find the way to enlightenment, we first work on developing some understanding and knowledge. We then develop our attitude so that we may finally take action and put our ideas into practice in the everyday.

Gradually, your mind will get back to its natural state of clarity and luminosity. You take a little breather from the rush of daily life and create some space, connecting with yourself and doing a bit of repair work through various kinds of methods I will show you. You will really be able to check in with yourself and peel away the layers of ego, attachment and burning emotions that come between you and your essence, your true self, who still has childlike wonder at the preciousness of life.

In modern living, it is easy to fall into looking outside ourselves for everything, from material possessions to acknowledgment of our achievements and successes. We even begin to define our identities through the eyes of others; we take on roles and play our parts. We allow our moods to be influenced by others, and we search for happiness in all the wrong places. But now you will get to be yourself. When you understand how important it is to love yourself, then you will naturally be able to love your family, your neighbors and eventually all other beings.

EVERYTHING IS WITHIN

Along the way, you will begin to release grasping attachments and learn to let go of expectations, your desires and needs; to understand the great freedom of realizing that, at the end of the day, our hands are empty, but how wonderful that we are simply human beings.

This sense of letting go will free up your time and your thoughts to give you renewed energy. Imagine how much space there would be in your mind without all those worries, self-consciousness and what-ifs. You will begin to notice what inspires you; you will have the space and freedom to grow and stretch yourself, and then inspire others too. We will get to know your ego, that most fragile but overwhelming mask we all wear in life, gently stripping it away to get to the true you, to uncover what really makes you tick.

You will get to know your own gurus—those people who give you warmth and encouragement and who must be treasured. And equally important, you will realize there are some people who unfortunately are negative for you and you for them. Taking a step back from these influences, even a mental step back, will allow your own compassion and patience to grow.

You can then develop your attitude, the will to *be* good and *do* good things—to rejoice in the well-being of others and to be generous instead of only listening to our own desires, to show humility and patience, and to act with love and kindness. It takes great practice, as this is at the very heart of discovering your own way and enjoying life in the everyday, but *now is the time.*

Happiness never decreases by being shared. • BUDDHA

The secret of the uncommon path is that, by taking care of others, you in fact are looking after yourself. And to take care of others, you need to think of yourself and your own well-being, but doing so from a place of generosity rather than thinking always of what "I want" or "I need." It's a cycle of interdependence and connection; we need to take care of others in order to take care of ourselves, and we need to take care of ourselves in order to take care of others. Both developments are needed if we are to walk the uncommon path; we need to benefit one another. This is the understanding.

Walking the path is about sorting things out so that you can relax and get on with things joyfully. You may start with contemplating and then begin to practice, and it is with practice that you really begin to learn. The best lessons in life come through living it. Every day you try to be a little nicer to others, you become a nicer person yourself; step by step, little by little, this will be an effective practice in the long run, and it will make the bumpy road a little smoother.

It is only by understanding how important your life is that you will be able to answer the question of how to make it better, to find its meaning. And to do that, you have to free yourself from your rigid view of yourself and the world around you. *Anything can happen in the next minute; that is the beauty of life.*

Perhaps you are frustrated by aspects of your life; perhaps you often feel angry or nervous or have sadness, regrets or feelings of guilt. You may be searching for the meaning in your life, or have that nagging question, "Is this it?" You don't want to complain, but you find yourself doing just that, often over very little. Or you feel somehow that time is flying by but being wasted; there aren't enough hours in the day, yet you still aren't quite fulfilled—things just aren't right. You want to be brave and follow your heart, but you have many expectations to live up to, which keep you a little fearful of making the wrong decisions. It becomes easier to make no decisions or to just fill your day with busyness. But this is starting to take its toll, through stress or boredom, you're not yourself.

I hope that as you read this book, you will see that, while life is certainly full of challenges, you as a human being are *good enough*: no better than others, no worse, but *you*. And that you don't need to go looking for happiness elsewhere, because it is right where you are, right now. Everything is within. And rather than sticking Band-Aids on our suffering, we can uncover the true causes of our anger, jealousy and pride. We can begin to let go. We can exchange our knowledge with one another; we can all benefit one another.

I don't say we should try to escape from modern life, but rather learn how to complement and nourish the modern world with our actions; to remember that we all come from nature and, despite our so-called differences, deep down we are the same. I myself am optimistic about the "modern age," because I always say the years ahead are going to be better than the previous ones. This is what I feel, and I'd like my students and friends to feel the same way too. I'm not attached to the future—after all, I'm here in the present—but I think it's better to be optimistic, to have a good feeling about life. Then whatever we are going through as a collective has a reason.

Many people talk and think negatively about the future, that it will be very bad for everybody. There is great suffering in this world, but I prefer to think optimistically that the world can change, that there is a better way, through the sharing of love and compassion.

We have reason to be optimistic. The potential is already there; after all, we are lucky enough to be human beings. Believe in others and you will believe in yourself. This is our simple approach. I have been traveling around the world for a number of years, teaching and talking in many places, and during this time I have been encouraged by my experiences. Looking at the memories I have accumulated during these times, I can recognize some changes in my students. They have become more spiritual, and I think that this is a very good change, a very good step. This positive bug is catching on.

I'm not going to try and say this is an easy, quick-fix journey. I, like you, am just a beginner, and so I just do my best each day and look out for lessons. But I want you to remember that there is really only one blessing in life—to look at the world and one another with compassion, with a genuine understanding. From compassion springs kindness, generosity, patience and, of course, happiness. Asking for any other kind of blessing in life—for luck, for a boy or a girl, for money or success—all these things are temporary. Ask instead for a light so that you may see the world in an understanding way, and that's all you will ever need.

WHAT WE THINK, WE BECOME

If you really wish to develop your life, you must first develop your mind. When you listen to any teaching, you first have to relax totally and open up so that you will *receive* something. Any sort of container has to be open in order to get something inside. Otherwise, what do you get if you keep closing it? Everything just runs off the surface.

> *Let yourself be open and life will be easier. A spoon of salt in a glass of water makes the water undrinkable. A spoon of salt in a lake is almost unnoticed.* • BUDDHA

I know that with any teaching, we are tempted to ask many questions, but I encourage you to do so in a relaxed way, rather than getting caught up in debate over every last "but what-if." As you read this book and begin to practice its teachings, draw the questions you have into yourself, into your own nature. Let them sink in. This is the authentic way of asking questions and of getting authentic answers. The questions should be helping you get in touch with your own insight. Small questions that are asked once in a while along the way are very important. The questions should help you become more relaxed, rather than more rigid or contrary.

Just as aspects of modern life can become a trap, catching us up in a whirlwind of busyness and expectations, spirituality can become a trap too. If we rush into trying to do everything right—

following every ritual in the hope we will suddenly be enlightened rather than taking it gently and easily—we will be making enlightenment and happiness an expectation or a demand. We will be looking in the wrong places. Sometimes the ritual of performing spiritual practice overwhelms the practice itself, or we get caught up in practice before we know what path to take. I think it is good to understand that we are beginners—even childish, when it comes to our minds—so that we don't try to run before we take even a first step. It is better to do something very small and really mean it, because then you understand the scene of life, the meaning of life.

If you try to do too much without understanding first, you might start to question the point of doing this and that; you might set yourself up for disappointment, both in yourself and in others. But if you know that you are likely to have many wobbles and make many childish mistakes, then you can smile at yourself and the world. And if you can smile at yourself, then you will be less likely to fall into the traps of anger, disappointment or jealousy. You will take a lighter step.

Therefore, I do encourage you to always investigate any teachings before you follow. Relate the teachings to your own life. Can they help with a problem you have or help you find your inspiration? Nourish your mind with these questions and also bring your thoughts and knowledge down to your heart to investigate how you feel.

And while I encourage you to ask the odd question along the way, don't let them put you off practicing, because it is by putting ideas into practice that we truly begin to answer our own questions. Sometimes we can get so carried away with debating the finer points that we get lost and never make a start. Starting something can seem difficult; we feel as though we are blocked from doing positive things. But there don't seem to be any blocks when it comes to negative habits! The practice of good deeds, of generosity or meditation, for example, can feel like so much hard work. We think about what we want to do, and then nothing happens for years. Then, somewhere along the line, our positive intention disappears; even the thought of doing something positive disappears. Things might not be too bad, but we become lazy, just sort of roaming around, leaving everything to "fate." There's nothing wrong with this, but we never really get anywhere, and at the end of our life we may realize we have been wasting our energy and time, wasting life's opportunity. So I very much encourage you in your commitment. It is a gift.

So I want to express my warm welcome to you at the beginning of this journey. I welcome you from the depth of my heart. I have realized over the years that my gift in life is to offer encouragement to others. I hope that we may walk together for a little while to help further your understanding of yourself and those around you, to find your inspiration and develop your compassion. You need to bring your own motivation to the teaching, why you picked up this book in the first place. And when something speaks to your heart, you have to do it, and really put your effort into it, to challenge your bad habits, your negative views of yourself, and walk your own uncommon path.

PART ONE

The Uncommon Path

The way is in the heart.
• BUDDHA

There are many lessons that the Turtle Club remind me of as they gently walk the mountain paths. It is good to take some time to contemplate your life, both its ups and downs. To remember just how precious life is, appreciating everything we do have, rather than worrying so much about what we think is missing. I encourage you to take in the scenery of your life and of nature, and contemplate all the wonderful friends and loved ones you have been fortunate enough to walk with. Try not to load yourself down with your cares or your expectations but step lightly, enjoying each day of the journey. Take your time, don't rush, and you will soon notice what really catches your attention, what inspires you and what matters. Your heart knows the way.

Enjoy the Journey

It is better to travel well than to arrive.

• BUDDHA

Since the second Annual Drukpa Council finished, I have not had the chance to thank all of our monks and nuns for their presence and their hard work. I have not even thanked all the hardworking volunteers, but I think by appreciating themselves, if they know how to do that—that alone is much better than me thanking them, one by one.

I was very appreciative of everything at the second ADC. There were some complaints, some nice things, some accidents, some small failures, some people were very happy, some people were very excited, some people were very stressed.

Several people complained that we had fewer teaching sessions and too many cultural shows. Some people said that to have a concert was too much, and they had to walk out, as they felt it was outrageous and too noisy. I can understand what they are going through and I appreciate that at least they came and joined together. I appreciate their disagreement and their complaints, *because everyone is entitled to having their own opinions, which we should appreciate and respect. This is a tough and rough dirt road that we are walking on. But without being relaxed, you cannot be a genuine spiritual practitioner.*

This is the main reason why I keep saying repeatedly, like a nagging old man, "Appreciate and rejoice, without any expectation." It doesn't matter if people are nasty to you, it doesn't matter if people betray you, it doesn't matter if people don't even say "Thank you" to you; by appreciating everything around you, from happy experiences to upsetting experiences, your life would be so meaningful, full of understanding, full of happiness, full of joy, full of strength and full of fearlessness.

I wrote this diary entry after the second Annual Drukpa Council, where we come together for teachings, to exchange views and knowledge. It was a time that truly reminded me that life is all about appreciation. Because in the fast pace of modern life, taking time to enjoy the journey can seem like an indulgence we just can't afford. Our "to do" lists are forever growing, our goals becoming bigger and more shiny than ever. When did life become a race?

If we can catch our breath, take a look around, and begin to see our life with a renewed sense of appreciation, then the journey itself takes on rich color and depth; we begin to take in the scenery and all the details. We have the time to meet good friends along the way, to be there for them. We begin to feel so much more familiar with ourselves, so that we can recognize genuine happiness when it's right there, to know what inspires us. We no longer need to be wedded to particular outcomes. We are more open to change, to the flow and the ups and downs, because we know we'll do our best, come what may. We know we are fortunate; we know that, with all its ups and downs, life is good.

In order to find your own way, first an appreciation of your own birth, your life, is essential. A sense of appreciation changes the whole world. Without it, life is boring, people are boring, the world is colorless. And not only do you feel bored, you also feel discouraged. Think about that word, without courage; when *discouraged* we allow fear to take control or we lose our spark. You do not want to really do anything. Instead, you only want to sleep. Then laziness comes. Or you have so much to do but can't really think where to start, so you begin to feel stuck or paralyzed. You want to wake yourself up, but each day you fall back into the same familiar, if no longer so comfortable, pattern. You try to make yourself happy through acquiring more possessions, or eating and drinking more, staying out late, but really you are putting off getting started with your precious life. And think about when you feel inspired, in the flow of life, when you feel you understand the rhythm of the world rather than feeling out of step.

You need to know how important you are, how important this body, this mind and your life are. If you misuse your life or don't really know its importance, then it just feels out of balance, and things aren't right in your world. You can only make life better and more fruitful if you understand just how precious it is. We are here for the blink of an eye, so why not make the most of it?

As we understand the importance of life, then we realize that now is the time to do good, to help and inspire others, especially those less fortunate than ourselves. Our appreciation is an awakening and, in turn, becomes our motivation.

Your Precious Life

We have a lot of good things in this life. You can appreciate the fact that you are walking, sleeping, eating food, that you can look and recognize people with a burst of warmth in your heart, you can listen, you can care. Think of all the little bits and pieces of your life that you have to be very happy about. Your body is precious. Your talents are precious. Life is precious.

If you have this kind of appreciation deep within you, then you will find your way, and you will feel moments of enlightenment in even the most mundane details of the everyday. Life is fascinating! Also, happiness, genuine happiness, comes from appreciation. You feel fortunate; you feel relaxed and savor each moment.

When one door of happiness closes, another opens; but often we look so long at the closed door that we do not see the one which has been opened for us. • HELEN KELLER, WE BEREAVED

Often we look for happiness in the wrong places; in what we don't have. Our complaints send happiness into hiding. We think about the things that are missing in our lives, rather than all the wonderful reasons to be happy right here, right now. "I don't have this, I don't have that, he did this to me, she said this to me." It's like when you are trying to be healthy and you only think about all the foods you can't have, rather than the wonderful array of foods that are on offer to you. Or you might find that you have a tendency to overindulge if given the chance, whether it's food or material possessions or in seeking out excitement and pleasure. And when you overindulge, you never quite enjoy the experience—it loses its shine, or that you are eating a great deal of food or spending, even wasting, lots of money because of some nervousness or unhappiness deep in your mind. You have to eat and eat, spend and spend, but your appreciation has been lost. You search for comfort but somehow can never quite reach it, because you're looking in the wrong place.

When you have a real hunger and you have an empty stomach, then your senses become heightened, you savor every mouthful of a piece of bread, you eat mindfully and appreciatively—joyously. It is not because that specific piece of bread makes you happy, it's because you know how to appreciate it—that is what makes life so different. You notice the little details in your day from the moment you open your eyes, which means you want to get up and enjoy the day, rather than turn over and hide under the covers.

The foolish man seeks happiness in the distance: the wise grows it under his feet. • JAMES OPPENHEIM

Like so many, you have probably been encouraged to have many goals through your life to aspire to and work toward. It's certainly good to work hard and be active, but there is a tendency to look only where we are going, rather than where we are right now. Everyday appreciation is about enjoying every step of the journey, taking your time to have a look around and see the beauty in life— in a smile, as you touch a loved one, as you contemplate nature, or get lost in your work, as you sip a really good cup of tea, or simply take a moment to completely relax and let the world go by.

For me, I feel that happiness is about appreciating even the difficulties you are going through because they are all lessons as you walk the path. In fact, appreciating your life is the best investment you can ever make, because this will eventually make you such a happy person that, even when the worst situation happens, you will be fine; you will be still calm and content.

When we have appreciation of our lives, then we have plenty of things to do and plenty of time to do them, because there is no nonsense in between. There are many people in this world who think they do not even have enough time to eat. Many of my students say this; they are so busy, but actually they are not genuinely busy, their lives are just full of nonsense. They are like slaves to all these things they think they have to do, rather than looking after themselves.

It is a lack of appreciation in your life that allows the nonsense to come in. Life may feel chaotic, you may feel pressed for every minute of the day and perhaps not particularly happy. You might feel as if you are running and running but not really going anywhere. You feel like a nobody, a ghost of yourself, struggling to find your direction. There is a common throwaway comment many people make that is such a strong sign things need to change: "I have no life." I find this very sad; life is so rich. But the fact that you are on this journey shows that some part of you understands, that you want your own life back so that you will be able to have plenty of time to do plenty of good things. And when you find things that you truly appreciate, you want to share them rather than try to keep them for yourself. Even as you breathe, you begin to give your appreciation out to the world through your breath, your happiness and health.

THANK-YOU NOTES

Why not begin a list right now of the everyday things in life you appreciate and are thankful for. Perhaps find one thing each day that you can ponder either as you wake up or as you relax during the evening. It could be anything, from your child's laughter to a stranger holding open a door. Look for the good in life and, like anything, appreciation blossoms and creates more with a bit of nurturing. You will begin to see things with an appreciative eye. You will want to make the most of all your opportunities in life, and gradually you will even see the helpful lessons that come through daily challenges and obstacles.

What Is Happiness?

We all want to experience some happiness along the way, but we're often not quite sure what happiness is. Is it the pleasure from a particular experience, being with a particular person or in a particular place? Is it selfish to feel happy? Can we make happiness a permanent fixture?

We are often so busy running around, wanting happiness, we don't see it right in front of us; it is like dew on the grass—there for a little while, but then gone. As soon as you get some happiness, the feeling disappears just as quickly. As soon as you get some pleasure, it too disappears, like those droplets of dew, or like chasing a rainbow. This is our usual pleasure-based experience of happiness, and we waste a lot of time and energy trying to find it. But relaxed and peaceful, long-lasting happiness can certainly be attained; it is quieter than our glimpses of heightened sensory pleasure, but still rich and deep.

Happiness is a perfume you cannot pour on others without getting a few drops on yourself. • RALPH WALDO EMERSON

Happiness is what bonds us all together. We all have the equal desire to have happiness, and at the same time we don't want to feel pain or sorrow. And yet this is something we rarely think about or truly understand. By remembering that every single other person wants the same thing, we can begin to understand happiness as something full of compassion and generosity, rather than as a selfish search for pleasure, for fulfilling our desires. As the Buddha said, "Thousands of candles can be lighted from a single candle, and the life of the candle will not be shortened. Happiness never decreases by being shared." Happiness makes you a good human.

For me, I think happiness comes with appreciation. Happiness comes when we are completely inspired, when we are intimately connected with something that moves us, something that really catches our attention. Wanting to improve our understanding about anything, even in a small way, is very good. Learning makes us happy. For example, I wanted to learn French, as I felt I couldn't communicate with my French students at all well, and this made me a little bit down. As I started to learn the language, I had a tremendous joy, as my understanding improved. As we improve our understanding, we improve our wisdom and are able to do things more skillfully, to the benefit of others. Remembering this helps you in your motivation. If you can continually be learning from each day to the next, with motivation to give something to others and to the world, then happiness will stay by your side.

Happiness Comes from Within

We might easily assume that certain things or people "make us happy," but happiness is about how we respond; it comes from within. A person can have many excuses for being happy or sad. You can be happy because your friend is with you, you have eaten some good food, or you are having a good time. But happiness—and the same is true for suffering—is not something that can be given by anything else. The mind is the one that gets happy, or suffers. External things are the trigger or the support, but the actual feelings have to come from within ourselves.

Think about when you find yourself immersed in an activity, or reading a book, or gazing at a painting. You feel beauty in that moment, and often you are spurred into some kind of generous action as a result, whether you are helping others through your work, or simply telling a friend they must read this wonderful book. When you are inspired by something it has a cumulative effect; you too want to inspire.

That is happiness; to be dissolved into something completely great. • WILLA CATHER

I also liken happiness to being "relaxed," because for me relaxation is true joy, as it feels so peaceful. It's why I like contemplation so much, it's like swimming in a deep ocean and gives me a deep sense of understanding—not so much sensual bliss, but an inner, gentle happiness. For me, this is what love means.

In today's frantic world, it is easy to dismiss this kind of relaxed happiness in the search for adrenaline and desire. But if we are frantic in our search for happiness, how likely are we to find it? If we think only of ourselves, we might experience a quick "high," but think of the richness when happiness can be shared, when it comes out of a connection with someone or something, out of a motivation to see the world in a good light. When you smile, your mood actually improves. Sometimes we don't even know why we're happy, we just are, and this kind of happiness is wonderfully infectious. Think of a baby, gurgling and chuckling to his heart's content when he wakes up in the morning. Even before he has the words to express his joy, it's obvious for us all to see. I think babies are as amused by their own laughter as much as by the sight of us pulling faces. Next time you catch yourself just smiling, think what a great thing that is, and, while you're at it, don't forget to pass it on.

Happiness wakes us up and makes us aware of even the smallest details, in life and in the world around us. Claude Monet said that he found his true inspiration in nature and, instead of keeping it to himself, he shared that inspiration through his painting, a true gift to all of us. There is so much inspiration for happiness to be found in nature; look at the generosity of the honey bee. The honeycomb is a thing of engineering beauty; how could such a small being create such a masterpiece? And then as the bee goes about its day collecting nectar to make honey, it helpfully transfers pollen from one plant to another; what an act of generosity. Many crops in the world are still pollinated by the humble bee. I think this gives so many people great happiness and inspires them to do all they can to help save the bees; they are so precious.

GROSS NATIONAL HAPPINESS

The tiny Buddhist kingdom of Bhutan sits in the Himalayas between its colossal neighbors, China and India. A few years ago,

Bhutan came up with the most inspiring idea: to measure their success as a country, not through the usual Gross National Product, but instead through Gross National Happiness. The idea is that government programs are to be judged by how much happiness they produce rather than by economic benefits. The aim is to better create the conditions for the "pursuit of happiness." They started with the voluntary resignation of the very popular king and the holding of democratic elections, as democracy empowers individual responsibility, which in turn is well linked to happiness. Community vitality is included among the programs, as are time use and psychological well-being—not the typical government programs, but areas that are intrinsic to modern life and happiness. Just think, how people spend their time is considered more important than how they spend their money. How people support one another within their communities is put high on the agenda because the accumulated effects are so beneficial to all—less crime, better care for the elderly and less able, a genuine sense of looking out for one another.

Ever since happiness heard your name, it has been running through the streets trying to find you. • HAFIZ OF PERSIA

Doesn't happiness often come when we least expect it, when we aren't looking for it? We often think that to be on the right path, then we should somehow be positive and happy at all times. But, of course, life is both happiness and suffering, joy and grief. If we didn't know suffering, how would we know happiness? I say if we feel good today, then great; if not, it's also OK. Don't try to fool yourself one way or the other, but honestly contemplate your own personal ups and downs. There is no need for you to keep these secrets; reveal them to yourself. That may sound strange, but unconsciously we keep many things even from ourselves. We don't investigate our thoughts, but rather keep things on a superficial level, which is really a state of "not knowing."

I was asked once, after a talk I gave, how people could "be positive" while also accepting whatever happens, even preparing for the worst. How could preparing for the worst be something positive? I think there is a great deal of pressure in the modern world to always be positive, but is that very honest? Bad things do happen in life, and sad things too. Indeed, the only certainty in life is death. Should we just put these away in a box, rather than let them free in our minds, where we can turn them over and try to understand them? To strengthen our minds and be prepared for anything that may happen is not to be pessimistic; it does not mean we *expect* the worst. As I will explore later, it is better not to have expectations at all, as they are really like invisible chains. The best preparation is to do our very best today and not try to predict what will happen tomorrow.

If you haven't wept deeply, you haven't begun to meditate.
• AJHAN CHAH

The Buddha called these ups and downs "the cycle of suffering," which can seem quite negative at first. But it's good to be honest, rather than try to cheat ourselves and pretend that everything is perfect; that way we are setting ourselves up for inevitable disappointment. It is easy to fall into the habit of wasting so much time finding everything in life that is "wrong." People say it's best to complain, to be honest. They say that if you don't, then you are suppressing yourself. When people say these things, I always keep quiet and smile; I'm not going to argue. I agree it's best to be straightforward and genuine, to be authentic, but the question I would ask is: Where does it start? These negative complaints can begin to pile up, and then all the good things are hidden and cannot be recognized or appreciated.

When we really begin to focus on this, to spend a little time at the beginning and end of the day thinking about these ups and downs, then our compassion will begin to develop too, in a natural and genuine way. We no longer hide away from mistakes and mishaps, but see the lessons in our day without beating ourselves up. We don't need to hold on to everything so tightly; we can lighten up. And as we begin to know ourselves a little better, this also reminds us to look for our similarities, rather than our differences. So that person we might feel frustrated with is having an up-and-down day just as we are. Compassion won't come in a big wave all at once, but as our appreciation of the details of life grows, so too will our understanding of ourselves and others.

Love yourself and watch—
Today, tomorrow, always.
▪ BUDDHA

REVIEW THE DAY

Lie down on your bed, close your eyes and put your palm on your heart. Ask yourself, "What has been happening today?" Let your thoughts come through your heart, and you will begin to get a sense that you *know* and have an interest to find out more. What lies at the center of your life? Look at your experiences squarely and honestly. I'm not here to say put a positive spin on everything, but to just accept them for what they are: moments in time, some that made you feel good at the time, some that gave you varying degrees of suffering. It is being honest with ourselves that is the key and investigating how we feel with a sense of compassion and acceptance for who we are; leave your judgments to one side. You really need to know the basic cause of things happening in your life. Life is a series of experiences of all types, and if you can look at all those experiences with genuine compassion for yourself, without blame or embarrassment or anger, then you will begin to know how things are and how they have developed.

Your Precious Body

The human body is like a boat, and it's our job to navigate the stream of life as best we can. Or you might see your body as a guest house: without it you cannot survive and walk your path, but also you cannot take it with you; at the end it is left behind. I like to say, therefore, be decent to your body and show it the greatest respect that you are able. It is the same as the way we treat friends, enemies, possessions, everything. By taking care of your health as much as you can, you are very decent to this guest house that is your body.

Somehow, over many generations, we have lost the connection with our body. We think of it as less than precious, unsatisfactory in many ways, if we think of it at all. A natural love and respect for our bodies has been replaced by a growing sense of disinterest for some, or something to be rigidly controlled for others, rather than a relaxed, nurturing relationship. We're not quite sure anymore how to relate to our own bodies; either we compare them to others and find faults, or we take them for granted rather than taking good care of them, because that would take time and effort we just don't have enough of. We battle against the natural aging process, forgetting that our bodies, just like our lives, are like rivers and streams, constantly flowing, constantly changing.

Take the relationship between what we eat and our health. This is widely recognized throughout both the West and the East, and yet obesity continues to become ever more prevalent, especially as countries encounter rapid modernization. It is as though we have lost the connection between our precious bodies and what we feed them. We hardly know at all now where our food comes from, even though it is all in some way, originally, from nature. There is very little that is recognizably natural about much of the food we consume. It has been through so many processes between the farm and the plate, and perhaps that is why it is easy to become less than mindful about what and how we eat.

When you see food growing, if you are able to pick a tomato straight from the vine and taste its sweetness there and then, you are reminded of how wonderful it is that nature provides us with this food to keep us healthy. Not only that, but food wakes up our senses, especially when we savor every mouthful. Many people don't even feel they have enough time to sit and eat anymore; we eat on the run, in our cars, at our desks, making phone calls or sending another message in between mouthfuls. And because we eat mindlessly, we hardly know when we are full; and we begin to eat for reasons other than looking after our precious bodies. We search for comfort and happiness in food. Yes, food should certainly make us happy, but in such a way that we become closer to nature, rather than in a grasping, greedy way.

Mind and Body Connected

Think of all the incredible things your body does day to day: you walk, talk, listen to your friends; you see in glorious detail through all your senses. And think of how your body connects with your mind: your heart beating faster as your loved one approaches, the warmth of caring touch, even the flow of feel-good chemicals as your body thanks you for that jog. Think of how stress affects your body, how your state of mind makes you feel. How does your body feel when relaxed and calm? What are the signs of contentment? If you can cultivate all of your senses, then you can truly appreciate the beauty in the world and in those around you: you can smell it on a warm, rainy day; you can listen with true attention and savor every cup of tea.

From the beginning of the pad yatra until the end of it, I had been fighting with different sorts of obstacles. I am proud to say that, after fighting a few weeks with these challenges, I have won them over. First, I developed an upset stomach the day we started the pilgrimage; it was very bad until yesterday. It bothered me every day; when I was walking I could not even look around, if I looked around, I felt like I would fall down so I always had to have one eye on the road. If I started to enjoy the view surrounding me, I began wobbling like a newborn chicken that had just hatched out of the egg.

Also, we were doing daily practices outdoors in −15 degrees. Not only me, but all of my friends said they couldn't feel their own fingers or noses, and they had no strength to use their lips to chant because the temperature was too cold. I was freezing too, but we managed it every day and night. Thanks to Rigzin and Lotus, our suffering was greatly reduced. Whenever we experienced this kind of freezing cold, they miraculously came out with hot tea, and it was a great joy to see those big pots. I could see everyone smiling in the cold. Most days we take a cup of tea completely for granted, but during those days, at an altitude of 5,000 meters, freezing, experiencing −15-degree cold, we savored every warming sip. I don't know how to thank Lotus and Rigzin enough for arranging this kind of warm hospitality always at the right moment. As I sit in my luxurious room where I am right now, I can honestly say I would be more than happy to be back there.

If you can appreciate this wonderful, beautiful body that you have been given, then you will also begin to appreciate your inner self—your beautiful mind and your beautiful heart. You set up a cycle of taking care of yourself so that you may be able to go about your day with the best possible energy. If you are feeling good and comfortable in your body, you are more likely to feel good and comfortable in your mind, and in your whole being. They are all connected.

If we are decent and respectful of our bodies, we will take care without becoming too attached to our own beauty, or strength, or worries that we are not beautiful or strong enough. If we spend all day admiring our reflection in the mirror, what kind of happiness does that really bring us? Tomorrow we may not look so good, and our confidence may suddenly be shaken because we're only taking care of the surface, the superficial. If we can appreciate and take care of our precious bodies from the inside out, then it will show in the twinkle in our eye, in our relaxed, warm smile, in our touch.

Take in the Scenery

Nature is painting for us,
Day after day,
Pictures of infinite beauty
If only we have eyes to see them.
• JOHN RUSKIN

We all come from nature and are a part of nature; *we are nature.* Even as you sit and have a cup of tea, you are taking nourishment and comfort from leaves grown perhaps thousands of miles away, or those picked from your own back garden. Nature offers us so many reminders about how life is precious, it makes us receptive, it cultivates our senses. When we think life is just horrible, if we walk with nature for a little while, we are often able to broaden our view and see life in a different, better light.

Nature doesn't worry about the past or race to the future; day simply becomes night and then day again, everything connected and evolving at the same time. Even in our urban environments, taking time to look around and enjoy the journey from one place to the next will often result in noticing things that surprise and delight us.

Taking in the scenery of life as we go along is all part of our appreciation. And the more we look around, the more we begin to get to know what inspires us, what we really like. Nature also has a way of bringing us into the moment and into our body, sometimes to help us contemplate, and often to help us let go of our worries and get back to the basics.

Sometimes people ask me very strange questions, such as, "Why do you like to organize or encourage your friends and students to do so much difficult *physical* practice?" I normally just smile. People ask many questions. Centuries ago, we didn't have all the modern machines that make our life so convenient, but what has this convenience done to us? Physically, we seem to be better off. Whenever we see old photos of people walking on a dirt road or doing very hard jobs like washing clothes with their hands, we feel that we are very fortunate. But are we better off inside? We are more restless, our mind is like a wild being, it cannot sit still, we cannot be peaceful.

Modern technology and communication means that we now spend so much time in the virtual world that it is easy to lose our connection with nature. I myself end up looking at the computer for hours, and yet often little is achieved; it is a true challenge to one's powers of attention. We cannot simply sit still and quiet in our surroundings without pulling out our phone or sending another e-mail. This is far from calming or comforting; our minds whir away, just like our gadgets, on permanent alert, flitting from one thing to the other. It becomes difficult to focus on just one thing, just this moment, what we are doing, or who we are with right here in the present.

The term *virtual* is the perfect description, because this modern world of technology is so illusive, it isn't real. Some of my friends even plant virtual trees or have virtual pets, which sounds cute, but I think there is a bit of a dangerous side to this too, so it is good to be aware. I know people who have thousands of "friends" they have never even met. We have to be the boss with technology and not let it take control of us; we have to be careful and mindful.

CHECK IN WITH NATURE

The minute you go to the office or step into your home, what do you do? Do you connect with those around you, do you go into the garden to feel the breeze of nature or enjoy the colors of the flowers, the trees or the sky? Or do you jump on the computer or phone to check if you have any e-mails or messages? If you live in a city, you might easily miss the changing seasons, but if you take a little time to look, you will draw it all in: the colors of the leaves, the smell after the rain, natural sunlight on your face. If you can slow down to connect with nature, you will find yourself connecting more easily with others; you will find your patience and humility. You will walk into work or into your house with a lighter step, with the energy of nature rather than your own agenda or anxieties. Nature connects us back with the present and reminds us, in this moment, that deep down, life is good.

Nature provides a wonderful way to balance out all the technology in our lives. This is why I organize the *pad yatras*. As I said earlier, *pad* means "foot," and *yatra* means "journey." I love this terminology very much, because for me it has a deep and profound meaning in the sense of grounding ourselves. One of the main reasons for taking a pilgrimage is to connect with our own innate enlightened nature through contemplating in the vastness of nature around us. This kind of walking meditation gives our restless minds a break. While a car can take you quickly to a physical destination, your feet can take you much closer to your spiritual home. Walking helps us to build a genuine and deep relationship with nature, with the nature of our mother earth. You can enjoy the scenery without analyzing or intellectualizing. Being with nature—climbing a mountain, listening to the sounds of a waterfall, getting some fresh air, and smiling at yourself and your friends—I think that's a great part of life.

Last weekend I dragged all my nuns, hundreds of them, for a pad yatra *to Gokarna, one of the highest mountains in the Kathmandu Valley. It was a meditation exercise to bring our physical self closer to our inner self, an active form of retreat. And then, of course, we picked up so much rubbish along the way. You would think that these mountains would be very clean and peaceful, but, sadly, people do not always appreciate the natural surroundings, and we came across many plastic food wrappings, water bottles and nonbiodegradable waste. I was shocked. Unless the minds of people change and all of us learn to improve our inner being and understanding, our environment will never be clean. I think a lot of education is needed so that we can all contribute to make this world better, greener and happier.*

I took the opportunity to try to inspire the villages not to use disposable cups, plates and bottles, and in fact I think I should discourage them from offering packed drinks or foods to me in the future. All these packaged foods and drinks are such a source of rubbish. I am very happy being offered traditional tea, tsampa *and local food. I even think the dietary changes in some places that I visit may be causing weak health. Local food is nutritious, good for*

our health, and doesn't cause unnecessary pollution to the environ-
ment. We should all try our best to promote that. So one of my main
missions for the pad yatra was to encourage local people to appre-
ciate their own culture and their own beauty, including the beauty
of their food.

From Phanjila to Hemis we collected 60,000 plastic bot-
tles, 10,000 chewing gum and tobacco wrappers and 5,000 cans.
I could not believe my eyes; if remote places such as this could be
full of that much rubbish, I wonder how many more times rubbish
we city people accumulate every day.

All the elements in nature and all living beings are our friends
and our supporters if we know how to interact with them positively and with understanding and appreciation. This is also the
same with our self nature. If we forget to connect with ourselves,
we lose touch and start feeling a little lost as we get into trouble.
Like those who love gardening, taking care of the flowers and the
plants, creating beauty, we have to take care of our inner self nature so that we might radiate creative beauty to benefit others.

My mother has had ill health ever since I was born, but through
her peaceful mind she does not complain; she is always smiling and
taking care of others. Pets, flowers, trees and small children are her
favorite companions. They all love her spontaneously, including the
flowers and the trees. Ninety-nine percent of the plants that my
mother nurtures will certainly grow. Even if she plucks a branch
from a dying tree and replants it, soon it will be growing beauti-
fully. I wish all of us had this authentic love and understanding to
cope and work with in our life. We would have an easier approach,

even in the face of unavoidable difficulties. Well, we can practice;
we can all practice.

I really think that gardening is a great thing to do, not only because I love the trees and the plants, but also because I think, through the gardening, we learn to appreciate the nature of the earth. Not that I am much of an expert gardener myself, unlike my mother, but I feel very fulfilled doing what I can. I know that my nuns love it too, when we landscaped the area around the statue area of Druk Amitabha Mountain, I could see they all enjoyed this too, even though it was hard work. We were all suffering from the harsh weather and heat, but we all had smiles across our faces. We even did our very best not to kill any bugs while we were gardening, which I was happy about. If we garden carelessly and selfishly, only for the sake of beautifying our own garden, it will take the lives of many others. We might create something superficially beautiful for the world, but those tiny beings will experience a big catastrophe; it will be like an earthquake for them. If, however, we can garden in harmony with nature, then I think it is so much more beautiful all around.

So nature helps us to connect with ourselves and to understand that we are all connected. As human beings, we see the consequences of our actions in nature, from our own gardens to how the world is doing right now. We see how racing toward a future, thinking of our own desires and needs, is putting great pressure on nature's resources. But if we don't ever stop to catch our breath and take in what's happening around us, we'll carry on regardless. If we can't respect nature, how can we respect ourselves? That is why I talk about ecology so much because I see such a strong connection between how we treat nature and how we treat ourselves. Because as soon as you take that moment to stop and enjoy the view, you begin to care about your own life and, in turn, everyone else's too.

Look into your heart.
Follow your nature.
• BUDDHA

Walking Together

Let us be grateful to people who make us happy; they are the
charming gardeners who make our souls blossom.

• MARCEL PROUST

A long the path, we meet many people. Our parents will often be there to give us a helping hand at the start, and it's good to walk along and chat with our friends and loved ones, to share what inspires us, and lean on one another every now and then for support or guidance. We take care of one another, become a guide once in a while, and sometimes need help with finding the way.

Good friends, teachers and masters, if you are lucky enough to meet them, must be much appreciated. If you have a good friend, then sooner or later they will in one way or another help put you in the right direction. They will indirectly or perhaps directly shape you into a better way. Even if you are behaving badly, they may help you solve problems, dispel delusions and help your inner confidence grow. Then the real happiness will come from within—within yourself. This is what a genuine teacher or friend can do for you.

Sometimes, when I talk to my students about the things they

can improve on, the way they live life or treat others, they become disappointed and upset rather than taking these comments positively. As a teacher I have always thought it is my responsibility to point things out, but of course I don't want to create disharmony between myself and my students, so if they stop listening, I have to stop talking. I understand that it's always easier to hear your teachers and friends praising you all the time, even when you are on the wrong track. I have to often tell myself that those who caution me about my missteps are the ones who genuinely care about me, so I must value them a great deal. Those who are diplomatic and always agree with what you say may not always be genuinely helpful. It's human to like to listen only to the people who say nice things to us, but it doesn't always help us grow.

Friendship is so important, I feel very sad whenever I see people who are friends becoming disappointed with each other because of small things. Good company increases compassion, loving kindness, wisdom and peace of mind, decreasing your desire, jealousy, hatred and pride. A friend can be a teacher; this person might be an ordinary being but can be considered a guide, someone who gives great support as you make positive changes. Once you have found someone you know to be a guide, you must value them highly and treat them better even than yourself, because a positive friend is equivalent to a great master or a Buddha. Value them from the depths of your heart.

You should be very careful when you look for a friend. Some people have negative influences; others have positive influences. But these influences from your friends are always with you. In my mind, this is the bottom line of all relationships. Think of how strong your intuition is when you meet someone—it does not matter if they are a complete stranger or you have known them for years. You can literally feel their energy. Is it happy or sad? Peaceful or agitated? Do you want to give them your warmth or happily receive theirs? Or perhaps you detect the need to just slightly keep your mental distance. Don't dismiss this intuition; your body may often be more aware than your busy mind.

It often is your teachers in life who open up a space and create moments of understanding, when the clouds in our minds part to reveal absolute warmth, tenderness and learning. It might be in a moment of comfort, either through their words or their touch. It might be that you allow these very special people to strip away your layers of ego, gently and with kindness, through laughter or by seeing beyond the labels, accepting you simply as you are, no conditions attached. We may find a friend or mentor particularly inspiring, one who helps us develop our cause and find the work we are meant to do. Inspiration is a great gift, as, once truly inspired, we cannot help but inspire others, to pass on the gift.

Positive people will tend to be close to "the nature" of the world; they have a great deal of respect. They respect their parents, they respect animals, the trees and plants, and so they respect their friends. If someone doesn't respect their nature, then often they don't even respect themselves. They may have a hollow appearance of acting as though they love themselves, but it is brittle, and can easily crack and break. But if you find someone who is filled with a feeling of understanding, then respect them, and you will too be closer to the true nature. These are the people in whom we find we can take refuge; to help calm our wandering mind. They embody the inspiring spirit of encouragement and so must be treasured.

If the traveler can find
A virtuous and wise companion
Let him go with him joyfully
And overcome the dangers of the way . . .

• BUDDHA

My beloved father is a master for those who need him for guidance on their path of life. For me, it has been a great gift being his only son. I have never felt lonely in my life, despite having gone through a lot of difficulties in my younger days, and I now understand that it was he who gave me the strength to pass through all the difficult periods. I do not think any one of us could possibly think of being as good a father as he was and is to me. When I was a child, he used to come up with lots of toys that he made from the parts of broken watches, radios, tape recorders, et cetera. I never liked those other, commercial toys. When I was a bit older, he had boundless energy and patience to play for hours with me, running after footballs and Frisbees and the like. He would push me up this long hill on an old three-wheeler bicycle so that I could ride down, all day long. He wouldn't give up entertaining me, even on rainy days, picking up both me and the bicycle in his arms and making lots of noise imitating a four-wheel-drive jeep struggling with a steep and muddy off-road climb.

I always liked horses and, after I became more of a man, he often caught wild horses from the mountains for me to stroke. Sometimes he even put me on the back of one if it was not too big and ferocious. My father has given me so much. It is such an honor to have not only a holy but loving father like him, and I feel honored too when I realize just how nice a father he is.

My father was recognized as the reincarnation of Vairotsana

when he was eight years old. I think he had a very hard childhood, as his parents did not accompany him from this time. He never speaks of the hardship, but, happily, I have gathered that with the moral support of my mother and the genuine love they have for each other, his life has been very much filled with joy and peace. I always thank my mother from the depth of my heart for being so genuinely loving and understanding for the sake of our family, and I am thankful that my father appreciates this and cherishes it. What a great combination they are.

> One day Ananda, who had been thinking deeply about things for a while, turned to the Buddha and exclaimed, "Lord, I've been thinking—spiritual friendship is at least half of the spiritual life!" The Buddha replied, "Say not so, Ananda, say not so. Spiritual friendship is the whole of spiritual life!"
>
> • SAMYUTTA NIKAYA

A nice community will also keep you in good company along the way. Talk to people; after all, if no one else knows where you are going, then your own interest may also begin to drift. Motivation is like a drum that someone is playing continuously; it is the rhythm of the world. If you walk only in silence, then eventually it might feel as though there is little point in carrying on. So take people with you, so that you may gossip and chat every now and again, make each other laugh and smile, keep each other going. Perhaps we are walking together for a little while as you read this book. I hope I may divert your good energy in the right direction!

The Teacher Within

The ultimate teacher resides within ourselves. Just like those people in your life who can offer genuine guidance, your inner guru is also there to help you find the way. You might think of this as your intuition, your soul, your heart or your inner compass. When the weight of expectations is on your shoulders, it can be hard to hear your inner teacher, or to know if what you are hearing is really from your heart or clouded by burning emotions or attachments that are controlling your thoughts and feelings.

As you begin to recognize those people in your life who are truly positive for you, you also begin to know and trust yourself again. Your natural confidence will begin to blossom, and you will find things become a lot easier, even during very challenging times. You may still have those times when you want to curse yourself for making the "wrong" decision or making a mistake, but you'll find yourself more resilient and quicker to pick yourself up, dust yourself off, and move on without the need for self-blame and recriminations. When your ego, which we will meet in the chapter Step Lightly, makes all the decisions, the potential for upset is far greater, because your ego is so easily hurt or put on the defensive. One word of criticism and the ego either crumbles into despair at the horror of not being perfect, or puffs itself up into aggression and dismay: "Who are *you* to criticize *me?*" With your much more relaxed inner "guru" inside, you can actually listen to criticism, and if it's helpful—great, you learn a lesson; if it has come from a place of ignorance, then you can politely ignore it!

Let Go of Negative Friends

Unfortunately, there are people in this world who are not so good for us, who unwittingly mislead us by creating anger, hatred, jealousy, desire or misunderstanding. I say "unwittingly" because the feelings these people trigger are only projections of your own negativities; and so, even negative people are our teachers once we become more aware.

An insincere friend is more to be feared than a wild beast; a wild beast may wound your body, but an evil friend will wound your mind. • BUDDHA

It is important to learn to recognize and then deal with these negative feelings. "This person is causing me anger, causing me desire, making me ignorant. Maybe I should leave him, silently, without saying anything." And if you are able to leave, think also, "I must develop my own strength so I can fight my negativities; otherwise I will find someone else like him again. There will be no end of bad company."

It can be tricky to always stay away from negative people, either because you may enjoy their company in some way, or you may have to deal with them in everyday life like a colleague. If these people had scary eyes and a fierce appearance, we'd find it easier to steer clear, but often they will feel very charming and attractive to us on the surface. How many people exclaim after the end of a relationship that they always seem to go for the "wrong type of person"?

Think of the times in your life when you have fallen under a negative influence. How were you during those times? Did you feel like yourself, or perhaps a negative version of yourself? Perhaps you even punished yourself in some way by staying close to that person—negative influences will bring out negative perceptions of ourselves, and then, caught up in a negative cycle, we might begin to act out that role we have created or put upon ourselves. Our own natural and strong self-esteem and confidence begin to be eroded or are hidden away beneath the layers as we begin to believe we are just bad or weak in some way, even though deep down we know it has something to do with someone who is misguiding us. Of course, even then we blame ourselves for being influenced, rather than realizing and accepting that some people just aren't good for us.

. . . But if you cannot find
Friend or master to go with you,
Travel on alone . . .
Rather than with a fool for company.
· BUDDHA

The good news is that often we have many very positive friends in our lives who will help us see what is going on and take a step aside from our negative feelings, to realize we have lost sight of our true self. You will then begin to be able to check whether your loving kindness and compassion decreases through contact with this person. If wisdom and compassion go down because of this connection, something is wrong. If anger, desire, pride or jealousy increase, something is not right. These are the two checks to see if this person you are with is negative or not.

On the surface, many relationships are seemingly OK: "Oh, you know, he is a pretty nice person." This person may be looking after us on one level, but it is helpful to ask, "does their companionship give me support in order to grow some wisdom, to develop my understanding, compassion and loving kindness?" Or, is it the other way around? Does it somehow work in a negative way, encouraging anger, ignorance or desire to grow? Sometimes this is very subtle—somehow the energy of a relationship causes you to go down spiritually. It is a difficult question to ask, but also very important.

We should never force people to stay with us. Sometimes, I feel that every relationship is like a marriage; if it lasts, that is fantastic, but if it doesn't, we should be appreciative that we have met and made a connection. What I am sad about is when people leave us with some sort of misunderstanding and carry with them a great deal of sadness, regret or anger. I always feel that letting go and rejoicing are very difficult practices for many of us.

Equally, it is our own inner self that can become a negative companion along the way. We have a tendency to get trapped by this mental enemy that comes from within. When the mind is influenced by this negative companion, then anger, desire, jealousy, pride and all the manifestations of our selfish ego grow rapidly. The majority of us have to live to some degree with this companion, and so it is important to be aware and also create an antidote through appreciation. The negativities in our mind are what undermine us and cause so much unnecessary suffering. But as we look around for all the things in life that we can appreciate, as we look to those in our life who reflect back our growing wisdom rather than our negativities, we can begin to leave our negative inner and outer companions behind.

> Do not look for bad company
> Or live with men who do not care.
> Find friends who love the truth.
> • BUDDHA

One Step Leads
to Another

Do not pursue the past.
Do not lose yourself in the future.
The past no longer is.
The future has not yet come.
Looking deeply at life as it is
in the very here and now,
the practitioner dwells in stability
and freedom.
We must be diligent today.
To wait until tomorrow is too late.
Death comes unexpectedly.
How can we bargain with it?

• BUDDHIST SERMON

As you sit here, reading this book, the world around you is changing, minute to minute. The leaves on the trees may be just coming into bud or turning color before they fall, the light is changing, as are your thoughts. Since the minute we came into this world, we have been getting older by the second. Just like anyone, I do not want to get old, but we have no choice—everything is impermanent. Nothing stays exactly the same, and so neither do we. We may grow up labeled as a "shy" person, for example, but there's no reason for that to always be the case. You are not the same person you were yesterday or you were as a baby, but, likewise, you are not different either. You are just you, someone who is continuously developing and growing and changing, moment by moment, especially if you *allow* yourself to grow and change.

It is very freeing to release yourself from the constraints and worries of time. And I know this is a big issue with people rushing around all over the place, feeling that there aren't enough hours in the day. We spend so much time worrying about what we have or haven't gotten done in our lives, we forget to enjoy the actual experience; we are caught up, anxious to achieve, constantly pushing ourselves to the next destination without taking in where we are right now.

Letting go of worries about time might sound lazy. Surely we all need to look to the future in order to be prepared? The message I want to get across is to begin to give up on all the *nonsense* with which we often fill up our time. When you don't have time to eat breakfast or lunch, are you really spending your time wisely? Are you relaxed and focused, completely in the flow of your task, or busy worrying about what happened yesterday or might happen tomorrow?

Freeing yourself from the constraints of time will put you back into the action, the real genuine action. It's not a case of being laid-back and doing nothing. You are not giving up on life; rather, you are giving up all the nonsense. You have the freedom to find what inspires you, what you really want to do with your life. You will be motivated to work harder and make things very creative. Past experience is just an experience, but the present is very important because it is the source of the future, so, to make the future fruitful, we need to look after the present. Today should be the source of a better tomorrow.

If I know I will die tomorrow, I can still learn something tonight.
* TIBETAN PROVERB

If you look at this impermanence from a positive angle, it means that nothing is impossible in this world. Everything changes from moment to moment, nothing and no one has a fixed identity, and nothing stays the same. Impermanence makes life much more interesting and challenging. It also means it is entirely up to us to decide what we want to do with our life—to have a new life, to have a beneficial life; we are our own boss and fully in charge of our destiny. Anything can happen.

Then the richness of life comes. You can clear away all the clutter and create a fresh, new chapter, one where real creativity starts.

To see a world in a grain of sand,
And a heaven in a wild flower,
Hold infinity in the palm of your hand,
And eternity in an hour.
* WILLIAM BLAKE, "AUGURIES OF INNOCENCE"

Embrace Change

Appreciating the fact that *everything is impermanent* helps you develop a deep understanding of your own life and the interdependence of all things and all living beings. Human beings often fear change, and yet we have no choice; we cannot stop the river flowing, and I would say that is a great thing.

When you realize that everything is changeable, you can then be comfortable and can adjust yourself to the rhythm of the world. You enjoy your friends and family, and yet you don't expect them to always be the same, to always have to fit in with your own view or your own wishes. You feel more alive and alert to the changes, but don't judge them—everything is prepared for. Negative emotions like anger naturally begin to take a backseat as you appreciate each moment, rather than worrying about what's been and gone. You begin to question whether you will feel this angry later, as you know nothing is set in stone, nothing is permanent. This gives you a bit of time, some space in which to develop control. You might not stop anger coming in the first place right now, but you control your actions, your speech. You won't speak those harsh words.

Nothing is shocking, or too exciting, just very comfortable. But you can also accept that, while today you might feel very good, tomorrow may be more of a challenge. To accept life's ups *and* downs takes a big weight off your shoulders. You learn from your experiences, whether they are happy or sad, and you are able to go through them fully accepting and appreciating them.

Let Go of Negative Habits

Some people feel their habits give them comfort, maintain the status quo, and keep things ticking along. But we often become slaves to our habits, just as we are slaves to the labels we put upon ourselves or we allow others to create for us. We're not confident we have the will or even the desire to change; why not take the easy option and carry on as normal? But, of course, it's not the easy option in the long run to continue with habits that restrict us or even bring us pain and suffering.

An example of this might be that we are in the habit of eating for comfort every time we have a difficult day, or we reach for alcohol to take the edge off things. Perhaps we are in the habit of being a nervous person, or always being the life and soul of the party. Our ego embraces these habits as they keep us under its thumb, believing ourselves to be a particular person who does particular things, when the reality is that we can be anything at any time.

Understanding that change is a completely natural part of life makes it a little easier to give us the motivation to make changes too. Although we might think habits keep things familiar and easy, they are often more likely to tip us off balance than keep us in a nice equilibrium and on the middle path. So people who eat or drink for comfort will often eat or drink to excess, and then feel really bad about that, full of guilt and regret; and equally, someone with an extreme "healthy" habit might shut themselves up in a box, unwilling to look around and try new things. Often those with a happy balance will tend to be in the "everything in moderation" camp, which is a very good metaphor for life.

Everything changes from moment to moment, so why spend so much time and energy worrying about what has been or what is to come? Why try to control time, those people close to us, or even our own lives? It's impossible. This theory is very important, both in meditation practices and in living our daily lives in a more lively, peaceful and happy way. It's good to take things easy.

Developing this little bit of knowledge will help us a great deal toward that path. Just a small change in your mind will make a tremendous difference to your life. We constantly walk a line between the lessons of the past and the uncertainties of the future. Every moment is relative to the previous and the next, in a continuous flow. Living in the present may at first strike us as selfish or superficial, but once we have made our commitment to acting always in the interests of others, then freeing ourselves from the anchors of time is extremely liberating, and it means we can get on with so much more.

See the Whole Picture

With this fluid and open perspective you will also find that, in any given situation, you can see the whole picture, rather than being "stuck in your ways" and seeing only from your own viewpoint. Eastern medicine is very much based on this principle. Practitioners won't simply take one symptom and treat that very specific part of the body. They will view the symptom in relation to the patient's whole body and also their state of mind, seeking to understand how the illness relates to the whole, and hoping to discover the true cause.

With an understanding of impermanence and the interrelatedness of everything, people often find that situations that previously created a boiling feeling of anger can be reacted to with gradually increasing levels of patience, and either a desire to connect and inspire change or to realize that tomorrow things will be different. There can be a worry that patience might be a form of cowardliness, laziness or not caring: "I can't change this situation, so I just won't bother to get involved." Action is still the key, but to act in any situation with calm clarity, versus anger and fire, is far more likely to yield a positive result, and is much better karma, in the long term. Try and look at someone or something in anger, and the reality will always be hidden by your own emotions.

It is important to understand how to take every movement, every change, every thought and every appearance as a true teaching. It is helpful, I think, to take some of the ideas we are exploring, for example, and see how they occur in our life around us. If we are able to do that, then we are really beginning to walk the path. This is the time to pause and reorganize our life, by reorganizing our motivation. The thing is that, if we are still alive, we always have the chance. Don't wait anymore; tomorrow is too late!

MEDITATE ON SUNRISE OR SUNSET

Nature gives us many teachings, and the lesson of impermanence is a great one. Day turning into night and the changing of time, the breeze, the sound of a waterfall, the waves in the ocean, the sunset and sunrise; all these give you a complete teaching about your own changing emotions and about relative truth. If you are on a beach, why not take a little time to meditate with the waves. How does one become another; watch the tide gently come in or go out, think of the vast ocean and how every drop is related to all others.

The trip to my good friend Venerable Master Hsin Tao's Ling Chiu Mountain was very inspiring. Ling Chiu Mountain means "vulture peak" in English. It is located on a cliff facing the ocean, so we can hear the sounds of the winds and the waves almost all the time while there. If we can contemplate these sounds, and the silences in between, we will be able to understand the nature of life and impermanence, which is just like the waves.

Understanding Karma

I always thank my karma whenever something good happens to me, such as meeting old friends and students, and seeing that they are healthy and happy. Karma is often a little misunderstood in the modern world as something very mystical and related to fate, but we Buddhists do not believe in coincidence, and we do not believe in luck.

It is simply a matter of cause and effect. Every action and even every thought has an effect, a consequence. It is easy in the rush and bustle of our busy lives to forget this and pay little or no attention to a great many of our decisions and choices over the course of a day, to forget that they matter, that *everything* matters. Unlike the concept of fate, karma is not rigid, and so we can all make a difference.

Literally, *karma* means "actions." Whatever you do is included in karma, no matter if it is a physical, mental or spoken action. Of course, we take so many actions while blind to karma, but as we become a little closer to our own nature, to our wisdom, then we will understand the good and bad effects more clearly. A person who is a little closer to her wisdom will not be carried away so much by ignorance, which is often the case in day-to-day life. We rush around, not really aware of everything we are doing— walking in ignorance, talking in ignorance. We are always on the move because of ignorance, even in our dreams!

The first step is to begin to realize what we are *doing*. This transformation in our awareness will help to replace ignorance with wisdom in our actions. We will listen more to our natural wisdom, instead of only our intelligent or egoistic mind, allowing it to grow and function in its own beautiful way.

The message is that we are all here to serve others, in whatever way we can. Our mind should always be vigilant and ready to act for the welfare of others. So, for example, something I personally like to support is the planting of trees, and people will ask, "How does that help?" I don't know why I am so interested in tree planting; I think I am a nature lover. For me, when you plant trees you are helping them to grow, to survive, which is also helping life to grow. Growth itself is life. You see your own child growing every day, and planting trees is a similar process. It is so beautiful when you see things growing like this. Trees then give oxygen to people. If there are no trees, there is not enough oxygen, and you get landslides, there is little rain, and people suffer. If you don't care about consequences, you just cut the trees down; as long as you have wood for your fire, wood to build your house, you don't care about the disasters that will affect society. We human beings can be so strange—we destroy our own virtues, as when we cut down trees rather than taking care of them.

When we understand that everything matters, then we begin to behave in a thoughtful way, thinking about the consequences of our actions and how we might benefit others. When we are careful, then good things follow, one after another.

Karma Isn't a Blame Game

Sometimes people feel the need to blame misfortune on some great being or the universe. Instead, we have to understand that it's our own karma and carelessness. Through this understanding, rather than blaming all our bad luck and misfortunes on someone or something else, we need to work hard and we need to be mindful of all our thoughts and actions to make sure that these misfortunes will not happen in the future.

I realize that karma is a difficult idea when we think about how often bad things happen to very good people. But as with everything in life, our karma is not just our own, separate from everyone else. Our karma is collective and interconnected with all others'. In Buddhist philosophy, this collective karma even goes back many generations, as we have all been here before and will visit again in the future. From a more mundane perspective, modern science says we are influenced by past generations by inheriting their genetics and traits, and we will influence future generations by giving them our genes and traits. So you see, we all have the karma of the world in our own hands. That is why we mustn't hide away or think of ourselves as somehow separate from others. We are *all* human beings. Of course, we all come from different backgrounds, but we are connected by our karma. Since we have this great karma to meet, we should be supporting one another and encouraging one another. This spiritual path that we are walking is full of bumps and potholes; we have to carefully hold hands with warmth, sincerity and understanding. Nothing is impossible when we walk together.

For the sake of this short life, we unfortunately tend to do all sorts of things that create bad karma. To get a nicer home, more money or more pleasure, we may act selfishly, pushing others out of the way in our rush to be the best, to serve our own happiness. We are all looking for happiness, but by putting our own ahead of others', we accumulate a lot of bad karma for the world.

If we understand the rule of karma, then we may stop and think before we act selfishly for our own happiness. Should we put our own short life first and accumulate all this bad karma, or should we think of others and the lives to come and do our best to put out as little bad karma as possible? We may only be here for the blink of an eye, but the way we live our lives will stay with the universe forever.

When we are able to stop, pause and think more about our actions, words and thoughts, we begin to see the cause and effect more clearly. We then begin to understand that, by changing the cause, if it is in our ability, we can change the effect. You might notice, for example, that if you can put aside jealousy, then you are less likely to speak harsh words to that person or feel pain yourself. And equally, by showing great joy in another person's well-being or happiness, you will feel a warm glow yourself. This is why we talk so much of love, compassion and kindness to others. Once you begin to be truly mindful of acting in this way, your love, compassion and kindness will give your words and actions great color and very good karma.

Step Lightly

Do not carry with you your mistakes.
Do not carry your cares.

• BUDDHA

There is an old story I would like to share with you about a
Zen master and his young student.

*The master and young monk were about to cross a river on
foot, but before they did so, they came across a young woman on the
riverbank who wanted to cross but who was too small and fragile
to make the journey. So the kind old master carried her on his back
across the river. This upset the young monk a great deal, as he felt
his master had violated the vinaya, the "rules" of the masters. The
monk kept quiet for a few days, but felt increasingly upset and angry
with his master as each day passed. Eventually, he couldn't help it
and told his master he was very angry. The old master laughed and
laughed, telling the young monk, "I left the woman the minute I
finished crossing the river, but you have been carrying her until now."*

What this story tells me is that we have to know when to drop
our burdens. It is easier to walk along the path if you are not

weighed down. You may need to carry food and shelter, but what else is really needed at the end of the day? We are also weighed down in life by many invisible but very strong ties. The past may hold on to us, or equally we may be attached to our expectations of the future. We desperately want things to be a certain way, to fit our view of the world, but we never know what's going to be around the next corner, so why try to always predict the future? We might be weighed down by self-consciousness, worried to try new things in case we make mistakes. Or we have such a fixed idea of our destination, that to end up anywhere else will lead to disappointment and a feeling of failure.

It is very human to care about certain things in our life, especially people, places and our achievements. We shouldn't think that having attachment is the same as having tenderness and care, such as the care we may have for a son, a daughter or family. It is very good to care about our parents, our business or our neighbors.

What's important is to begin to recognize when those connections support us and allow us to grow, when they give us momentum and inspiration, or when they keep us stuck, fearful, uncomfortable or even bored with life. Attachment is labeling somebody or something and then strongly believing in that label. As soon as we try to fix something or someone with a label, to put them into a box, then we create the possibility for hurt and disappointment if we lose it, if that person changes or we can no longer afford that house we wanted. If we allow a person to become "mine," we can easily feel jealous or angry if that person doesn't quite fit our idea of what we desire them to be. Or we might label ourselves, using our memories as anchors that tell us we can't do certain things or be a certain way, or desires push us to seek happiness in all the wrong places. If we can let go of such attachments, then we can walk with a lighter step and be a much easier person. We can go wherever our heart takes us.

Letting Go of Attachments

I am back in Hemis, the holy monastery where I spent many years since the age of seven or eight in spiritual retreats and trainings. Ladakh is the place I feel most at home. Every time I visit, I feel so happy to be here and so sad to leave. Although I know this is a form of attachment and it's not advisable to be attached to anything in this world, I can't help it. Many great gurus and holy dakinis have blessed this beautiful place, and they have left many of their footprints, handprints, stupas, palaces, statues, and all sorts of self-arising holy imprints for us to have a chance to be reconnected with our own primordially pure nature.

All of us need different sorts of inspiration and encouragement, especially places, monuments and people who can inspire us to do good things and be kind. I am so happy that Ladakh is here to help us with this. I want to welcome everyone to visit Ladakh and to fall in love. It's better to be in love with something good than something bad, isn't it?

As you can see from my own love of the place and people of Ladakh, I realize that as human beings it is in our nature to form connections, especially when we are inspired or encouraged by something, somewhere or someone. But exploring the degree and nature of our attachments with material possessions, places, emotions, expectations, people, the past, our experiences, and even our own ego and self-image are all very helpful steps along the journey.

Understanding comes when we begin to realize whether our attachments are positive for us and have a relaxed, joyful nature, or if they stir up more disturbing, "grasping" emotions in us. After all, there are so many desirable things available in the world, it is easy for the wealth and "goodies" in life to carry you away. Your life can become a bit of a whirlwind as you grasp for more. And so you have to learn to apply a real sense of patience. You will never be able to have a peaceful mind if you have strong, grasping attachments. Instead, you will tend toward feelings like jealousy or frustration. For example, you might get upset if someone else has more than you or a better reputation. You get caught up in comparisons, you might become anxious and full of worries, unable to think with clarity, spending your time wondering about others or whether you, yourself, are good enough, rather than getting on with your own actions, your own life.

But if you practice nonattachment within, then you will be able to take or leave possessions, you will be less fixed in your ideas, and you will understand that whatever kind of person you are on the surface, whatever kind of life you have, it is what is within that really counts. You don't need to give away everything you have and go to the Himalayas to meditate in a cave to find happiness or enlightenment; you can practice letting go right here, within the richness that is your own life.

You only lose that to which you cling. • BUDDHA

Attachment is literally a barrier between you and what you are trying to reach; a chain that limits both your thoughts and actions so that you can't stretch and reach your full potential. Have you noticed that rich people sometimes walk a little differently? They have a certain way of walking because of their pride; they are not very flexible, and so everything is stiff. When you are rich, it is even more challenging to be tolerant; you can't bend down, but this is the exact time to apply a sense of tolerance. There is the danger that you are literally married to the money—not to your wife, not to your husband. Human richness is not there—only money. But with growing knowledge and understanding, you can be tolerant and flexible, without any sense of snobbishness, however rich you are.

Likewise, just as there is nothing wrong with wealth, there is nothing wrong with having a good reputation for certain activities. But you need to learn to practice patience and not be carried away by this, not to let your pride grow wild. Pride will drive you far away from the place where you belong and be the cause of more pain. The ego boost of fame or reputation might make you think you don't need anything else: "I have everything now; the whole world knows me." But the bottom line is that you need your family and their support, just like everyone else—the support of human touch, human care. Whatever you needed before you gained your reputation, you will always need. That is a very important teaching for having a balance in your life.

At the end of the day, there is nothing you can take with you. Your possessions, reputation, relationships and your body are all eventually left behind. You only have one stomach to feed. Regardless of how long good friends and relatives live together, they must someday depart. Whatever you build, be it businesses or buildings, they will collapse at some point in the future. It doesn't mean you shouldn't care, but it doesn't make much sense to become too strongly attached.

I hope you will not think I am being pessimistic, but this is the reality we are in. And when we understand this, we see there is no point in being angry with one another, even when there are some people who are so provocative, causing afflictive emotions like anger. But when you give yourself time to think about it, you will know there is not much point in getting angry or irritated by so many things, because at the end of the day, we are simply left with ourselves—nothing else remains.

Once you realize this, it is much easier to be on everyone's level so that, even if you become rich, you can bend down to clean the floor, play with your grandchildren and serve others. I know it is hard to think of letting go of all those things we feel give us pleasure, our objects of desire. There are many things around us that we hesitate to abandon, that raise in us the question, "Why should I?" But those who manage to practice nonattachment toward their belongings, their bodies and their egos are the luckiest people in the world.

Attachments Create a Mind-set of "I Should . . ."

Being attached to a certain way of living may cause us to restrict ourselves; parents will even want their children to "settle down" to a more appropriate, prescribed way of life. It's no surprise that this kind of settling creates chains around people, and they feel weighed down by expectations and comparisons. For some time they might feel great, as they've handed over the responsibility of their happiness and life to some role they have to fit. But gradually, the weight becomes heavier, and questions about regret and fulfillment begin to arise.

Expectations kill the beauty of life, the beauty in the unexpected. They keep you so busy, running ahead of you so fast that you can hardly keep up. Expectations make you anxious; you live in fear they might not be fulfilled, you are disappointed if life doesn't live up to them and feel a sense of anticlimax, even if everything goes according to plan. You really don't give yourself a chance to be happy either way. This is why I say, have no expectations and then you will be fine with whatever results. It doesn't mean you have no direction or motivation in life, that you aren't optimistic or excited about the possibilities, but you stop trying so hard to see into the future or force one version of the future to happen—you stop placing *conditions* on your happiness and free yourself to get on with today.

The good news is that we don't have to change the situation of our life to free ourselves; it's all a question of the way we look at things and our attitude. It's about cutting loose and being our own person, letting go of duty or guilt, and walking with lighter footsteps.

Releasing attachments will definitely help your understanding. When you face a big problem, decision or challenge, it won't seem quite so big, as you have already released it within the self; you have listened to your heart and made the best decision you can, but you are also accepting and aware that all you can do is your best. Being more free and flexible, you will adapt to situations as they change; you feel more prepared and a little more easygoing; you can see things from different perspectives, rather than from one fixed and rigid view. Everything is much more peaceful.

Possessions

Material possessions can trap us if we are not careful. They create a sense that things are "fixed" in the world when they are anything but—everything may change. Likewise, these possessions can have the effect of putting our own thoughts and feelings about what life is into a kind of box. Our ideas become square, rather than fluid and moving, as they should be.

We build a house and then say, "This is my house," and we are stuck with it. You almost become inseparable from the house, believing it to be part of you. We think of it as being forever, permanent, as if we can take it to the next life. We are too possessive. Of course, there is nothing wrong in having a house, nothing wrong in having wealth, but they are not a part of you. Your roots are not in your possessions; they are deep inside of you.

I have a friend who is a money broker. I don't know exactly what he does, but he's my student and has been practicing for many years. Several years ago, he and his partners faced tremendous business problems. Their bank collapsed and they lost all their money. Everyone suffered. The bank's manager jumped from the building and died, many of my friend's partners had heart attacks, and some had nervous breakdowns. Even now, he's the only one of them in good shape. I saw him just a couple of weeks after the bank collapse, and he was OK, comfortable. He was, of course, concerned for his family and business, but because he wasn't attached to his situation, it didn't impact on him in the same way as his partners. Frankly, I was amazed; I was even a bit hesitant to see him because I thought he might get so upset talking about it. But, no, he was smiling as usual.

If your practice comes from the depths of your heart, even

when extreme problems arise you will not collapse under their weight. You know that you will be able to take each day as it comes and walk on, rather than feeling your world has ended. It does take great practice, but we can always start small.

Burning Emotions

The easiest way to spot the emotions that have the potential to harm us and others is to think of them as "burning" emotions. Just think of anger, jealousy, pride and even desire; it is when these become heated that they cloud our thoughts, our compassion and our true selves. We literally become hotheaded; the anger or desire may burst out at the expense of others or sit inside us, bubbling away to the boiling point so that we can't think straight anymore.

Afflictive emotions—our jealousy, anger, hatred, fear—can be put to an end. When you realize that these emotions are only temporary, that they always pass on like clouds in the sky, you also realize they can ultimately be abandoned.

• HIS HOLINESS THE DALAI LAMA

Good feelings of love and passion can also make you care a great deal, can even make you cry, but rather than coming from a selfish source, they are born of compassion and a genuine concern for another's well-being. So, while you might become attached to lust and so feel very lonely if you are on your own, with true love you have a sense of freedom—you care for someone or something, but you are not controlled by those feelings or that person. Likewise, you are not looking to control or own them. As soon as you do, your emotions will easily become more burning in nature, making you feel agitated, uncomfortable and not yourself.

PRIDE

Pride is something you have to be careful of every day. You may look in the mirror and feel pride. Maybe you have nice-looking eyes or a good nose, and this gives you pride. There are so many things that can give us pride. Today this is often considered a good thing, confused with self-confidence. You are taught to be proud of yourself and desire the pride of your family or friends. "Go there, be proud of yourself, don't be shy, you are the best." This kind of teaching is why the world is becoming more chaotic; the forthcoming generation is going to have a very big problem.

It is a subtle distinction, but I would like to say that all these things you are proud of can be very nice, but you should let go of your pride in them. Beautiful things are beautiful forever, we don't need to invest pride in them, but simply let them be; let them be good and not have the potential to harm by creating jealousy or a grasping desire for more. If you don't have pride, you can have everything. Everything is OK because you have a sense of tolerance. But you have to be cautious of feeling arrogant and proud— proud of your body, your money, your name or your reputation. Just be cautious.

JEALOUSY

Like pride, jealousy is very sneaky and can come at almost any time. Anger and desire are not sneaky; we know as soon as they come. But, as pride can be confused so easily with confidence, jealousy can easily sneak into our daily life as we do our best to succeed. As we try our best, it is tempting to compare ourselves to others and become jealous of those who we perceive are doing better than us. Or as we cling a little too hard to a relationship, we turn everything into an excuse to become jealous; we can't quite just be relaxed and easy with our partner or our friend. Jealousy is a very severe afflictive emotion. It stops us from learning and growing, it creates misunderstandings everywhere, it clouds our efforts, so that even when we are trying our best, we are not enjoying life; it feels tainted.

ANGER

Anger is often described as a "red mist" that comes upon us, as if we are no longer in control of our emotions or sometimes our actions. Anger can overwhelm us, but equally over time and with practice, we can learn to control anger, to cool the flames and replace them with growing feelings of tolerance and patience instead.

Letting your anger bubble over into hurtful words or actions can certainly harm others, but the person it often hurts the most is you. Think of how unsettled you tend to feel after an angry outburst. I agree that it is not healthy to bottle up your anger inside, so that it creates a terrible and painful pressure that may blow at any time, but, if you do not learn to control your inner anger, then triggers will constantly appear externally; they will be never ending.

When we are angry, we often feel stuck; we can't communicate effectively, so we just roar instead. There is much anger within families, at work, and even on the bus or the train. Why does anger come upon us so quickly and with such force? Why are people in the Western world experiencing more and more anger when they have so much wealth and comfort? What have they really got to be angry about?

Remember that people with much anger are really suffering in their hearts; it is not a good place to be. For many, it is a case of taking life a little more gently and, when you see or feel just the very beginning of anger taking shape, you take a mental side-step and ask yourself if it will really help to explode at this time. Can you recognize your anger and learn from it without directing it at others? You can still care deeply; you can still make your point or protect a fellow human being from harm, but with calm strength rather than an uncontrolled outburst, which tends to have a negative effect all around. In time you will be able to look deeper than the anger itself to the cause; you can let go of that grasping feeling and *keep looking*.

DESIRE

Desire is like drinking salty water; the more you drink, the thirstier you will get. If you blindly follow your desires, it will drive you crazy so that you indulge yourself more and more, while at the same time your desire just gets stronger and stronger, never satisfied for very long.

Desire is a tricky emotion, as we often feel it is intimately linked to joy and love. But, although it can stir intense, pleasurable feelings, I encourage you to explore any feelings you have of desire. Are they grasping and wanting—"I want this, I want that, I want you"—or are they truly loving, without any attachments to them, not controlling in any way of you or the object of your desire? Think about that moment in a relationship when the intense, aching feelings of desire transform into something more relaxed and easy; that moment when you just know it's a good relationship and you can start to breathe again. Isn't it that moment that is full of true love and joy?

Abandoning negative desire doesn't mean that you have to abandon all things or all people that you like. It is about abandoning the grasping desires that you find you become too attached to, the ones that fuel a sense of greed or intensity. We can even become attached to pain, both emotional and physical. Scientists have shown that people who *expect* physical pain are more likely to experience it. I would say the same can be said in our emotional lives. Desire is often mixed up with pain, and often some part of us is attracted to this feeling, or we think it's our lot in life—that we attract emotional pain. Sometimes this type of desire or pain even tricks us into believing that this is what it feels like to be alive, when in reality, we couldn't be further from the truth.

As you get into the natural flow of your life, you will find these emotions burn with less intensity; that it takes a lot more provocation to fuel the fire, that patience and tolerance grow as anger and jealousy diminish. I think people often worry, though, that by calming their anger, or especially their desire, they will somehow lose a strong part of themselves; that to be hotheaded is to be passionate, to really care deeply about things in your life or other people. But, think about it—when you are burning up with an emotion, do you really feel like your true self, or as if you are perhaps a little possessed? You might want to get that feeling of release as you let your anger explode, but how do you tend to feel afterward? Do you really feel good about yourself?

When burning emotions are out of control, I feel we lose our understanding of both ourselves and others and are instead controlled by our emotions, by ignorance. I describe this as a very thick and strong darkness that makes it difficult to *see*. This can happen in the moment, particularly when we feel aggrieved by a thoughtless act, like road rage, littering, or rudeness, or perhaps we feel belittled by a telling off. Or the embers can be stoked over time—say, we are unhappy at work or in our relationship. In both cases, we become attached to our emotions. In our minds, someone has done wrong by us, and it's very hard to let those emotions go; it feels almost as though we are serving some kind of justice by being angry, or that we are showing how deep and meaningful our relationship is by being sick with desire. But do any of those burning emotions make us feel good? Do they get us anywhere except stressed and upset? Even our bodies react to these emotions, often through headaches, or stomach upsets, or a general feeling of agitation that makes our mind whir, our breathing shallow and our hearts race uncomfortably. Yes, we are human, and so these emotions are a part of us, but I hope to give you the tools so that you may give yourself a bit of time when they arise. Not to dismiss your emotions, but to listen to them and understand why you feel the way you do.

Create Space for Compassion

If we can develop our mindfulness in everything we do, then we will gradually begin to understand our emotions, where they come from, and if they are good or bad for us. It isn't easy in the moment to quell anger, fear, jealousy or desire, but if we spend a little time daily exploring ourselves and our emotions, then over time they will be less controlling. If you can recognize the "poisons," then you can take a good step toward making the path a little less bumpy. And then you will begin to be able to turn your anger into patience, refrain from speaking harsh words and rejoice for others instead of feeling jealous. You will be generous in your thoughts, hoping for the best for everyone.

In this world
Hate never yet dispelled hate.
Only love dispels hate.
This is the law,
Ancient and inexhaustible.
You too shall pass away.
Knowing this, how can you quarrel?
• BUDDHA

Letting Go of Your Ego

It is the nature of the ego to take, and the nature of the spirit to share. • BUDDHIST PROVERB

What exactly is this thing called ego? Well, in my mind it is just that, a constructed "thing" that we easily confuse with who we truly are. Our ego is our self-image, it's all the labels with which we describe ourselves, all the experiences that create our emotional triggers. It's the lens or the filter through which we see the world. For some reason, often we think it's set in stone, when, like all things in life, it's ever-changing and certainly needn't be something that we feel bound to or controlled by.

Over time, this construct that is our ego builds up layers of resistance to change and makes us self-conscious. From our earliest experiences during childhood and then throughout life, our ego tells us who we are and what we should expect from ourselves. It begins with how your parents described you as a child; say you were labeled shy and quiet and then played that role well into childhood, before realizing you are really quite chatty. Perhaps you were a "good" child, instilling an anxiety that one day, eventually, you would disappoint. Or you were a "nightmare," naughty and rebellious, so that you began to wonder if you would ever be "good." Of course, every child is so much more than one thing, but such labels tend to have great sticking power, and as you grew from a child into an adult, your ego grabbed on to them as strong identifiers. You might then have a tendency to be stuck in the past, with this rigid view of yourself and the world, anxious about how to let go and just go for things in life. Or you might find yourself often rushing headlong to the future, running away from the past so fast that you can't just be where you are.

When we let our ego take control, then our attachments to possessions and people, even to burning emotions, become ever stronger, like chains that prevent us from living our life with freedom and simplicity. Our ego clings to the causes of suffering. It prevents us from allowing our natural wisdom to function in its own, very beautiful way. We cover it up with layer upon layer of fabrications in our minds. So we need to cut through the ego; it needs to be taken and thrown away.

This can get confusing, because while everything in the world and in life is connected and interdependent, it should not be a controlling connection. As soon as we add the word *my*, then the connection becomes exaggerated. We exaggerate something or someone's attractiveness because they are *mine*, or we might exaggerate the unattractive qualities, often in ourselves. "I'm just not funny," or "I'm boring"—little things that go unnoticed by others become huge defects in our minds, become reasons not to let go and just go ahead and realize that today is a beautiful day.

A Strong Ego Makes Us Weak

The ego doesn't seem to like change very much. It tends to impose a rigid way of being and seeing things, which is why it is so easily hurt, often by the smallest prick, the smallest challenge to our own set of beliefs. And when our ego is strong, so too are our judgments of others and of our own thoughts and actions. The modern world is very judgmental, telling you how you are meant to act and look, whether you are a success or a failure, a good person or bad. Expectations placed on us by family or society, or those that we place on ourselves set us up to be constantly judged, and therefore to be often disappointed.

It is wonderful that children are taught to be confident in themselves, to try their best and know that they can give anything a go, to dream. But in recent generations, these very good intentions have often turned into creating a heavy weight of expectation as children grow up into adults. And with expectation comes a building up of the ego. We begin to feel entitled to certain possessions, to a certain level of what we consider success and wealth. Children grow up feeling they already know it all and become closed off to learning, exploring and discovering. The most obvious example of this is when a child grows up dreaming only of becoming famous. Without a good purpose, all this type of ambition can do is feed the ego, so that it will become increasingly more difficult for them to find themselves.

Ego is often mistaken for confidence, but the ego is really quite ignorant and creates many obstacles to our happiness. It is a real troublemaker. The "I" is a very strong and vivid thing that influences our life. I need, I want, I like, and so on. We place so much attachment on what the ego wants; if we can begin to let go of that attachment, then life becomes so much easier. For example, say we want to go somewhere, but if something comes up and we can't go, we don't regret it or feel angry; we do something or go somewhere else. *We keep going.*

Each person has inside a basic decency and goodness. If he listens to it and acts on it, he is giving a great deal of what it is the world needs most. It is not complicated but it takes courage. It takes courage for a person to listen to his own goodness and act on it. • PABLO CASALS

INVESTIGATE THE WORD "I"

As you go through the day, at first simply observe all the times you use the word "I" and investigate how you do so. What are you referring to? What does it represent? Are you letting your ego rule your thoughts and actions—I wonder what that person thinks of me, what do I think of them, who is better, more successful, more attractive? We are bombarded by thoughts that come directly from our ego, that balloon of pride that is so easily popped by even the smallest pin. Just observe this at first, and then begin to see if you can look beyond all the comparisons and doubts that are fueled by our egos and our fears, and begin to be yourself.

As we begin to see that nothing in this world is inherently real, but is in part a creation of our mind, it begins to help us strip away our layers of ego; it makes us less rigid and more open and accepting of what other people think or say. For example, you may think a person is beautiful, so you label that person as inherently beautiful. And then a friend comes along and says, "Oh, no, they are not beautiful. I don't like them." The reality is that neither of you is right or wrong, because nothing and no one is set—it all depends on the person looking. The mind is the creator of everything. This is why I think it is good to try and practice saying, "I think," or "I feel," whenever you can, rather than stating everything as an unquestionable fact. Then it is much easier to have a conversation and, if you need to, agree to disagree.

If we allow the ego to take control, it makes understanding difficult. Even though we are very learned, very clever and smart sounding, deep in our mind we are very dull. We do not know what is really happening, who we are, what we are doing, or what our direction is. We do not know, so we go on blindly. That is why sometimes I say life is a gamble. We might hit upon things that go well for us, but it is all a gamble. Hopefully, something good will happen, but we don't really know. When we live life in this way, we have to make many limiting presumptions to get by; we convince ourselves we are sure, rather than being open to whatever may come.

We Copy Everything!

When you think about it, we are always copying and comparing ourselves to others. We copy the way other people live, the way they eat or dress. If somebody else is wearing a new style of clothes, tomorrow you will go out and buy the same for yourself. If that woman is wearing this dress, it must be very attractive, so I should also buy it. We have forgotten how to be ourselves. Then, comparisons set in, we begin to judge ourselves to be better or worse than others. We get out our boxes again, labeling people, labeling ourselves, feeling jealous or proud, rather than simply content to be ourselves.

With our egos in control, we make a tremendous effort and use a tremendous amount of energy to try to manipulate things to be just right, but then what we have created covers the intrinsic beauty of our own nature. Fabrication always results in a lot of problems, and then disappointment follows because we were expecting too much.

Replace Ego with Humility

The key characteristic while practicing nonattachment is humility. Before we can learn anything and receive knowledge, we need to first lessen our pride and then become humble. This humility is developed through nonattachment. If you are still attached to your body, your looks, youth, wealth or whatever, there is no way you can be humble.

If you lack humility, your pride is like a big, round balloon.

Everything slides off; it can't hold on to anything. And because there is no substance, even a little needle can pop it. Pride is always the same; it's big, sometimes huge, but without solidity. It boasts, "I am this, I am that," enlarging its self-image. If someone says something our pride doesn't want to hear, it either falls apart under the merest pressure or puffs up and declares, "I am better than this person—who do they think they are anyway?"

Because of pride, you close the chance of receiving, while humility makes you open to everything. Whatever you want to know, whatever people say to you, you listen and accept.

Ego and Emotion

If you think about it, it is our ego that is often associated with triggering those burning emotions that ruin our day, and often the day of those around us too. None of them make much sense when we are feeling happy and at one with ourselves and the world, but in the moment they can be incredibly strong and not only affect the moment but create deep-seated insecurities; they are that playground of our inner self-critic, our wounded inner child.

Anxiety is running riot in the modern age—that underlying knot of unease, the feeling that things, or you, are just not quite right. For some people, anxiety fuels the image they have of themselves; that niggling doubt that you might not be good enough, or that you might make the wrong decisions. You are weighed down by your own impossible standards; you might be a perfectionist. You know deep down that no one is perfect, but instead of freeing yourself, you keep striving, heaping the pressure on. The ego loves anxiety because it keeps you in check, it relies on a fixed image you have of yourself that is often tied to the past, rather than relevant to the here and now.

Depression too is reaching epidemic levels in Western societies. I see a strong link between the great expectations people now have from such an early age and throughout their lives, and the increase in depression. During very challenging times, such as the world wars of the last century, people actually tended to be happier in their day-to-day lives, even when so many lost their lives. Their resilience was much greater, perhaps because they learned to let go of their expectations and take joy in whatever they could, in little moments.

Depression can be likened to self-loathing. Those who suffer will often even feel they are being very selfish in their illness, so they like themselves even less. It is a great sadness of the modern age that depression is so widespread. It needs careful treatment, but I can also see how it is fueled by the ego, because really it is a misperception and misunderstanding of the self that means you can get into a depressed state.

When the ego is in control, for some there is a great deal of self-consciousness, which in turn leads to feelings of embarrassment or even humiliation. *Humiliation* is burning. You feel so small and actually would prefer it if you could just disappear altogether. It is a feeling strongly associated with memories from early in our lives; that first moment when we were made to feel stupid or unattractive or unliked. The ego holds on to these memories and the feelings that went along with them, making it easier to feel them all over again.

It is not easy to calm feelings of humiliation in the face of bullying or when others are directing strong criticisms at us, especially as they often surface as physical reactions first, like feeling

hot all over or bursting into tears. Again, these feelings are linked
to not accepting yourself as you are—the feeling that sooner or
later you will be found out and your flaws will be painfully ex-
posed, that those early memories are right and you really are stupid, unattractive or unlovable.

Guilt is another of those emotions that your ego will try to cling
to; for me, it is an emotion trapped in the past. Taking responsibility and looking for a solution to a problem is a very positive step
to make, but holding on to guilt will eat away at your confidence
and hold you back from the helpful process of learning from mistakes and experiences. There's no action attached to guilt, it just
makes you feel bad. Parents feel guilty about not spending enough
time with their children, but so often they get caught up in the
feelings of guilt rather than taking a step to do something about
it. You feel guilty at work because you haven't made a phone call,
but rather than it spurring you on to pick up the telephone, the
guilt seems to paralyze you so that you spend all day thinking about
it and what the consequences might be. You hide away, when you
know deep down the best thing would just be to get on with it.
Can you think of a time when you have done this and then, when
you eventually got the courage to face the music, it wasn't nearly
as bad as you thought it would be?

As the ego so often looks externally for affirmations of self, it
often ends up in a blame game. Blame causes a great deal of pain
and little else; it doesn't do anyone any good, if you think about it.
Self-blame makes us feel we are bad or useless—we allow our
mistakes to control us rather than learning from them and letting
go. It is pointless to blame either yourself or others. Think—what
does it ever achieve? It is what you do next to help find a solution
that matters.

We confuse taking the blame with taking responsibility. Yes, we are all responsible for our actions, but if we try our best, then what more can we do? Blame is crippling, it stops people in their tracks, they become fearful of making the same mistakes again or making any mistakes at all, and so they'd rather sidestep taking any chances at all. Or there is a feeling that we need to apportion blame to others to somehow make ourselves feel better, so we can say, "It wasn't my fault." Does that ever make us feel better?

Shame is humiliation we put on ourselves; it's often related to guilt and self-blame. We are ashamed of our actions and so spend time wallowing in what we did wrong, rather than thinking, "What am I going to do now?" Like so many of these ego-driven emotions, shame keeps you trapped in the past and inactive rather than taking the next step. Everyone makes mistakes, but you can't turn back the clock—all you can do is learn and allow those lessons to help you today and tomorrow.

Sometimes the ego makes us cave in on ourselves, as when we feel shame or embarrassment and we want to disappear, while at other times it puffs itself up to completely unnatural and unattractive proportions. On the surface, arrogance appears to have a great deal of confidence, but it is a mask beneath which lies much insecurity. *Arrogance* is never kind, and if a person can't be kind to others, then how can they be kind to themselves? While anxious people will exaggerate their faults, arrogance often fools its own wearer into believing everything is just great, thank you. By its own nature, it's not something that a person can easily admit to being, which is why it is such a favorite of the ego. In fact, it's the characteristic we most easily associate with the word *egotistical*; the big "I am."

It is easy to see the fly on the other person's nose, while ignoring the horse on your own. • TIBETAN PROVERB

Arrogance is often partnered by *defensiveness* when feeling under any sort of attack. And often, just about anything feels like an attack to a person when arrogance is in control. An anxious person may crumble and retreat into their ego, while an arrogant person will fly straight back at you, defending their ego with cruel words to keep anything or anyone from getting to the vulnerability beneath the surface.

Ironically, when we go on the defensive, it is usually from an indefensible position. Our perfection has been questioned; deep down we know we're not perfect, but we can't quite accept that and go with the flow. So we spend time and energy defending a fabrication of ourselves, which is why defensiveness always feels so hollow and as though someone is standing on very shaky ground.

If you fall into the trap of identifying yourself in terms of how you compare to others, then your ego will place you, not only worse off than some, but also better off than others, leading to feelings of *self-importance*. The modern world is so competitive that this is extremely hard to avoid, but if you think back to times when you have felt better in some way than others, was it ever a very good feeling deep down? Because to raise your importance, you need to lower someone else's, which I think we know even at the time is unkind, but we fall into a habit of doing this.

It is always healthy to try your best, whatever your abilities, but when the ego grasps at competitiveness, it can become a chain around your neck; you are always looking forward, never content to simply enjoy the moment, never happy to just have a go. *Competitiveness* may well bring you material or intellectual success, but if you can't rejoice in the success of others, then you are missing out.

The modern world can teach us to be very *critical*, both of one another and ourselves. The ego loves to be critical, because it's another way of keeping things the same; some people will describe all the things they are not good at before they get to their perceived strengths. And it is easy for self-critics to in turn become very judgmental about others. That person isn't trying hard enough, isn't loving enough, isn't perfect enough. The ego often likes everything to be just so, and your whole being feels under threat a great deal of the time, because the reality is that things can never be perfect; you can never be perfect. It doesn't stop your trying, but, like competitiveness, it stops your living in the moment. Perhaps you did very well in your early school days—you were a 10-out-of-10 pupil. But then one day you got 9 out of 10, and it felt like your world would end. It sounds ridiculous now, but those feelings stick around, deep inside, and every day that you don't quite live up to your own exacting standards, you feel perhaps you could've done better. That's why I say, even as you read this book and look to make little improvements, the biggest gift I can offer you is acceptance. You don't need to be cruel to be kind; just open up your heart and be more accepting and less critical. Every person is valuable, so why do we interrupt so much or scold or judge? Enjoyment and happiness is important to everyone, not only to *me*. So let them be.

Our ego encourages us to look out for number one, fearful that no one else will. All of these characteristics are labels our ego clings to; they make up the story we tell about ourselves, but they also hold us back from being ourselves and living our life with a relaxed freedom. None of them make us kind or generous, none of them are a part of our true nature, however much we feel their presence.

You need to develop the ability to look at yourself and see your own nature, to know that you are simply who you are, doing your best each day, looking to where you can improve now and tomorrow. Don't waste your precious time and energy feeling guilty or regretful about the past, judging how good or successful you are as a person, in your work, in love. You are perfectly OK as you. And once you can truly accept this, you will begin to see the same is true of others. None of us is perfect—we're human beings; why keep looking for the bad when there is so much good?

Seek out that particular mental attitude which makes you feel most deeply and vitally alive, along with which comes the inner voice which says, "This is the real me," and when you have found that attitude, follow it. • WILLIAM JAMES

ASK YOURSELF, "WHAT SORT OF PERSON AM I?"

Some people are more suited to finding their way by thinking things through, while others are more physical beings who may need to literally take a step back from situations that provoke them. Some people are more sensitive than others, more excited, but then vulnerable to collapse and depression. They can get very easily irritated, angry, want to fight or hit out. When they get irritated, they don't give themselves time, they just go boom. On the other hand, some people can keep their anger in their pocket and practice patience. This is someone who has a little more strength of mind and so might be particularly suited to practicing contemplation and meditation. They will be able to take a mental step back, whereas others will need to literally walk out of the room!

So we have to check ourselves and ask what sort of person we are. Right now we often try all sorts of self-help techniques or practices, as if we were shopping in a supermarket. We pick everything up, and most of the time it is the wrong thing for our nature. It is like being a patient, and a particular type of medicine may work for someone but not for you. Different types of medicine suit different types of people, so we need to always be checking in with ourselves to find out what is right for us in all aspects of life.

I feel that many of us sometimes lack the courage to look at ourselves in the mirror, and yet we look at others with magnifying glasses. This is how we make ourselves miserable. Let us have the courage to look and see ourselves clearly. Knowing your own shortfalls is a fearless way of living, because only when you know these can you put your foot down and say, "OK, now I have to improve. I have to change."

The right way is to understand that everything is within yourself, and so work with yourself and develop yourself. If you understand that the mind is the creator of everything, then you will begin to feel that everything is in your hands. I hope that this realization feels like a kind of freedom; this is my own experience.

You do not need to leave your room . . .
Remain sitting at your table and listen.
Do not even listen, simply wait.
Do not even wait, be still and solitary.
The world will freely offer itself to you to be unmasked.
It has no choice.
It will roll in ecstasy at your feet.

• FRANZ KAFKA

Freeing yourself from a rigid image you have of yourself and those burning emotions that your ego would like you to cling to gives you a renewed resilience and flexibility. When objects are hard and brittle, like glass, they are more likely to shatter than something pliable. Introducing a bit of "give" into your life is a wonderful release from all that pressure you've heaped on your shoulders in the past, or had heaped on by others. It gives you the ability to take the ups and downs of life as they come, with the strength of adaptability, and opens you up to all the exciting possibilities. You will be more loving to your family, kinder to your neighbors and to yourself. You won't need to run away, but will be warmer, more understanding, more comfortable with the world. And the reason you have become so warm, so nice and so loving is because you have let go.

From Self to Selflessness

The fruit of being egotistical and selfish is to stay in suffering. The fruit of taking care of others is enlightenment. If we think about the attitude we tend to have now, in our everyday lives, you can see this in action. Often, what we do every minute of every day comes from selfishness. You may do something for your children, your parents or friends, but it's also for yourself. Even if we are giving, there is some kind of expectation too: "Oh, yes, I gave this and I may get that in return." We may be doing good, so it's not all bad, but we have some way to go. We need to realize our weakness and understand our selfishness. Then we can begin to change our attitude and stretch our minds. Because right now, the room in our minds is sometimes so small, we can't even be there. So we must expand our minds and let go of our egos by understanding how important happiness is for all beings. You already know that happiness is important for you. It's the key part of your life. Everyone wants happiness and no one wants sorrow. The first step along the uncommon path is therefore to really know how important happiness is for everyone, not only for oneself.

Spiritual practice is about training your own mind, your own inner self; it is not about training others. It is really about how much you are able to expand your inner space, so that "I" becomes smaller. If you have this notion of "I" and "others," and you can't stop seeing others' negative qualities, then you have a lot to work on. You have not traveled enough of your own inner bumpy path.

Slow Down for Clearer Vision

Write it on your heart that every day is the best day in the year.
• RALPH WALDO EMERSON

ooking back to the Turtle Club, I think the best part might be the gentle pace with which they approach our walks. While others race on ahead, they take time to get to know each other, they pause to look at the breathtaking views and notice so many more of the details. These days, I take the slow option while traveling and try to take trains from one destination to the next as much as I can. I must tell you, taking trains in India is the best experience you can ever get. This sort of journey will become a yesterday's memory very soon. Once rapid development takes over, once more people want to have quick journeys, the slow and noisy but beautiful and amazing trains that we can still find all over India will disappear.

In the train, we can experience so many things. We can see the different villages, we can talk with people sitting in other cabins, and we can buy some local delicacies and enjoy them if we have strong stomachs. The trains in India are known to have many varieties of food and hot masala tea. I always gain weight after a long train journey. If you are interested in practice, you can take out your *mala* and your holy text to do your own practice; no one will mind what you are doing!

I remember, when I was very small, I used to take train journeys in Darjeeling. Those were golden times in my life. I can still remember the smell of the burning coal, the *choo-choo* noise made by the train, and the company of different kinds of people. Even today, I still love to look around in the train—what are the people doing, what are they eating, what are they talking about, where are they going . . . ? There are so many activities to connect with one another, and there are so many chances to be connected.

Nowadays we connect less with people in this way; rather, we mostly try to connect through screens and buttons and find that many misunderstandings arise as a result. I say to everyone, don't stay at the computer for too long. Give yourself time and space to be connected with nature. The external nature will bring you closer to your own nature. If we keep looking outside for something, for happiness, for peace, for love, for luck, for bliss, we will never be able to find them, because they are all within us. If we cannot develop or find these positive qualities within ourselves, then we will always be affected by external situations. To have this inner development, we have to slow down, listen more, talk less, pay more attention to our inner voice, and pay more attention to the present, instead of thinking about the future and regretting the past. For us, most of the time, our mind is everywhere. Therefore we cannot appreciate even our food, our family, our job, our friends; forget about appreciating our own spirituality.

Mindful Living

If you can go about your day-to-day life with a little more mindfulness, you will find life infinitely more relaxing and rewarding. Mindfulness encourages appreciation, which in turn helps us to be more generous and kind to others, which in turn is bound to bring us happiness. With mindfulness you can make the most of even the most mundane of activities something to enjoy, like doing the washing up, and it will also help you to stop and think for a moment before you react to situations, before your anger suddenly bursts forth, or before you speak harsh words without thinking. And if you can make mindful decisions, then you will be following your path, taking your time to choose, but also accepting whatever may happen, because you are following your heart.

I don't wish for us all to become terribly conservative and abandon the laughter and spontaneity in our lives, or to become very slow in all our decisions or actions because we start analyzing and overthinking everything. The key with mindfulness is that it is about developing your inner awareness rather than allowing your thoughts to take over. It allows all your senses in on the act, and your heart too. Really it is about opening your eyes, taking a breath, seeing your world around you, and richly experiencing everything you do—from a walk in the park to dealing with a challenging person at work with patience and maybe even a little understanding, no matter how challenging they are! Wherever you are, whatever you are doing, you apply the skill of investigating your mind. It needs to be there all the time, in daily life, rather than something you bring out of the dusty cupboard just once every so often.

Let us spend one day as deliberately as Nature, and not be
thrown off the track by every nutshell and mosquito's wing that
falls on the rails. Let us rise early and fast, or break fast, gently
and without perturbation; let company come and let company
go, let the bells ring and the children cry—determined to make
a day of it. . . . If the engine whistles, let it whistle till it's hoarse
for its pains. If the bell rings, why should we run? . . . Time is but
the stream I go a-fishing in. • HENRY DAVID THOREAU

Awareness and Attention

As you develop attention during your every day, you begin to notice the details, and you notice other people more.

For example, when we walk past a homeless person in the
street, most of us don't even look. We don't care because we don't
see them. We might spare a kind thought, but it is the barest, fleet-
ing thought. What we need to do wherever possible is to receive
these situations as a teaching in compassion. Think about the possibility that, if tomorrow you were to become like this, how would
you be able to cope with it? Don't blame their situation on their
karma, but rather really put yourself in their shoes. When we take
our blinders off and look around, the great thing is that we are
strong enough to see, and seeing will make us stronger.

As you give your attention and awareness to a very sick friend,
for example, you will not only help them a little, but also you will
be prepared yourself if you ever find yourself in the same situation.
You will even be prepared for death, because you have looked at it
properly and contemplated what it means. You no longer hide from
it within your thoughts or within your heart.

A brahmin once asked The Blessed One:
"Are you a God?"
"No, brahmin," said The Blessed One.
"Are you a saint?"
"No, brahmin," said The Blessed One.
"Are you a magician?"
"No, brahmin," said The Blessed One.
"What are you then?"
"I am awake."

We cannot expect ourselves to be all knowing all of the time. But with alertness and attention, we can find out more. Say you fall blindly in love with someone, but she does not love you at all. You even live together, on the surface very much in harmony. But for some reason, she has been acting all these days, all these months and years. You didn't know, and even she didn't know what she was getting herself into. So you see that not knowing in itself is a great deal of suffering. You do not have to go miles away to understand what suffering is or read complicated texts. But you can begin to know a little more by being mindful of what truly speaks to your heart. Even as you read these words, don't feel you need to follow everything; listen openly, contemplate, try things out and decide for yourself.

No one can give you better advice than yourself. • CICERO

The Age of Multitasking

Nowadays people cannot even walk along the street without doing something else at the same time, such as talk on the phone, send an e-mail or read a book. People don't just meet to eat together but to negotiate or do business. Whenever our dining partner goes off to the cloakroom, we can't wait to check if we have any new messages on our phone, rather than just sit there for a few minutes, enjoying the fact that we have nothing to do.

I hope that you might find that you can simplify things a little and give each thing you do more attention, rather than always looking for the next distraction. If you are eating breakfast, savor that time and enjoy each mouthful; it's a wonderful time to reflect and create a sense of relaxed but active purpose for the day ahead. If you are writing a report at work, switch off all those other distractions for a little while so that you can really focus. It's easy to start ten things at once, but without focus, you'll struggle to finish even one of those things well.

With awareness and attention, you not only have more to appreciate in your day, but you also find that time helpfully stretches out, rather than making you feel hemmed in and always in a rush or a panic. As you focus on one thing at a time, you end up getting so much more done, and the irrelevant minutiae of life gradually takes up less and less space, because you are now so aware of what really matters.

When drinking water, think about the source. • TIBETAN PROVERB

Learn to watch and wait. Emotions come and go like waves on the shore, so if you can be mindful of them, you will understand where they come from and also that they are impermanent, like everything. If you are sad, even if you are really suffering, you don't need to become attached to that sadness. You can let it drift off, as a friend comforts you or makes you laugh; it's OK to let emotions go up and down gently, rather than trying to force them one way or the other.

We often live in a very head-driven world, placing all the emphasis on intellect; what do we think about this, what do we think about that. It is a good idea to remember all your other senses whenever you can during the day. Take your time eating, savoring each mouthful, every taste. Yes, stop and smell the roses, and look around you, at the people you know, at strangers wandering by—how is the world today?

If you are mindful, you can ask your inner self any question you like, however difficult, and you will know the answer.

PART TWO

Walking Your Path

If we are facing the right direction, all we have to do is keep walking.

• BUDDHA

It is first important to have the intention to practice something new; in this case, that might be living your life with compassion. But then some people wait for months or even years before they act on their intention. You have good motivation, but don't yet know how to turn those thoughts into action, to bring them into your everyday life. You feel that you will start later, you can wait a bit. You think, "I will try to practice," but then forget to do *anything. Talking is very easy, but your actions will tell you if you have improved or not.*

We might think that we can see our future: in five years I will have more time, my children will grow up and I will be able to practice. *This is our plan. But most of the time, our lives don't quite go according to our plans, so we should begin to practice right here, right now, without wasting a moment. The minute you get some understanding, jump into it. Don't worry too much about "what do I have to do?" Just be yourself, have a go, and bring the practice into your heart. If you find it challenging, that is good. If you just felt very comfortable all the time, it wouldn't be such a good sign. If things are challenging and you have a little bit of hardship, that is a good sign that you are really going through something and that you are alert and aware.* Your heart is awakening.

Develop Your Compassionate Mind

We are what we think.
All that we are arises with our thoughts.
With our thoughts we make the world.
Speak or act with a pure mind
And happiness will follow you
As your shadow, unshakable.

• BUDDHA

T o develop your mind is a great thing; it keeps you interested in life, curious and passionate. You want to learn each day, to stretch and grow. You can approach tasks with focus and clarity, become immersed and also know how to relax and calm your mind, to simply take in the passing clouds or look at the stars with wonder.

If you are hungry, then you will be inspired by food; you will appreciate it all the more. You smell it: "Wow, that's good, let's go and see what's cooking." The same is true for the mind; you need to be hungry for inspiration and knowledge. And then, when you know what you want to do, you need to set your mind to it, focus and don't get sidetracked. Consider, decide and then act; that is the essence of training your mind so that you can get on with the life you really want to lead. A distracted, directionless, scattered mind will keep you wandering off the path, following your wayward thoughts, while an inspired and focused mind will help you step lightly, with momentum and assurance, and allow you to spontaneously place your awareness wherever you choose.

Calmness, even for a few minutes, gives you the chance to appreciate life. It reveals life so that you can really see it. Right now we bury appreciation under the weight of all our busy thoughts; we are controlled by our thoughts, we run after them and can't sit still, either mentally or physically. But with a little stillness, our thoughts become more friendly. They listen to our inner hopes and help us find solutions; *the way*. They create a gap, a feeling of space in which we can become ourselves and begin to see the world around us with a bit more understanding.

Let distractions melt away like clouds disappearing in the sky.
• MILAREPA

The mind's natural state is clarity and luminosity, and this is what we Buddhists call Buddha, our term for enlightenment. It has nothing to do with a particular religion, nothing specifically to do with Buddhism; it means "universal truth." If you think, or if you believe, that the Buddha exists outside, separate from yourself, such as in the form of a statue or something like that, then I would encourage you to take a different approach and recognize that the Buddha is within.

There are two states of the Buddha mind; one is the purified state of mind or the *inspiration mind*, which shines a light on your way in life, showing you that you really can make a difference and make the world a better place in whatever way is right for you.

Because without an inspired mind how can you go for it? The second is the accomplished state of your mind, or the *practical mind*—in other words, your attitude so that you begin to desire to be good and do good things for others.

Right now, we have not realized the nature of our own mind, therefore we have to work on it and develop this realization. So often we read or listen without actually taking much in; it goes over our heads or just passes us by. We don't even *know* our own thoughts. As we begin to respect and understand ourselves, we become more open to what our daily lives and experiences are teaching us. We notice details with more clarity, and everything becomes so much brighter. Everyday lessons will really start to sink in as we open our minds and our hearts.

The Promise

The key as you begin to develop your focus is to always keep in mind the simple promise, to help others. This will keep your motivation pure and show you the right path. Different people want to help in different ways. In Buddhist philosophy, there are three main motivations; the first is that you want to become enlightened "for the sake of all beings." We consider this a *skillful* person, a leader or trendsetter who wants to develop and use their talents to help give others happiness or lessen their suffering.

The second type of person we call the *shepherd*. You want to help others reach enlightenment, and then you will too, like a shepherd who finds a good, safe place for their sheep, and then relaxes. This is a very *caring* person who has a great degree of compassion and loving kindness.

Those who have saved one life have saved the entire world.
• TIBETAN PROVERB

The third motivation is that we want to be enlightened at the same time as others, with them, not before them. We call this the *navigator* attitude, as in those who navigate a boat. They see a storm coming and try their best to cross the sea with their passengers. They don't think that they should go first and then lead, or that they should put all the passengers first and then go. They want to cross at the same time.

What type of person are you? Do you want to improve your skills and knowledge so that you might help others in some way? Or perhaps you are a nurturing or caring type of person who can use those attributes to protect or teach others. You might be a really good team player and would like to contribute to something that is greater than the sum of its parts.

Thinking about how you might best help is a very good step along the path, because often our common attitude is to tend to do whatever we do for ourselves first. Even when we do things for others, we often expect something in return. This is perfectly natural, as we are just beginners on the path, but we should always watch our mind and our motivation; if our mind and motivation are positive, then the energy we send out to others is also positive.

With our thoughts we make the world. • BUDDHA

The mind, like anything, needs looking after to work well. If you have a car, for example, that looks very nice and new in the beginning when you buy it, but you continue to use it without maintenance, its condition will deteriorate day by day. You need to check the brakes, the oil and the engine from time to time. This is the same as our mind; we have to check in from time to time, every day. If you don't put an effort into maintaining your car, even if externally it looks very nice and expensive, it will not work. If we focus all the time on our bodies and don't repair and watch our mind, after a time it becomes wild and uncontrollable. If your mind is disturbed, then life will be disturbed. Your nervous mind makes everything nervous. Rather than run away, give yourself a chance to understand the message your mind is giving you, the teaching. So, if we continually take care of our minds, then we will help ourselves to not be dragged down by the poisons of attachment, anger, ignorance, discouragement, pride and jealousy. We keep a lookout.

The Inspired Mind

We are all here to inspire each other and to inspire our own minds toward enlightenment. Being inspired creates a great space. Developing your inspiration mind opens up your heart, and you find you naturally choose to do things for the benefit of others; you act with compassion. As you develop your mind, you relax and contemplate what moves you, catches your attention and inspires you in your daily life. You discover where it is in life that you want to go, your direction.

When you lack inspiration in your life, then the opposite is often true; you might feel hemmed in and can't really think which way to turn. You might feel you don't have time to look at the world around you and so miss all the things that can offer you inspiration. Without inspiration, how are we to feel motivated to do anything worthwhile? Excuses pile up. When our minds become a whirlwind of clutter, there is no room to breathe, and we literally can't think straight. So, taking even a few minutes in the day to sit, watch and contemplate the wonder of the world is an excellent start. Then gradually you will find or rediscover what truly moves you and gives you your purpose. Open up your mind, open up your heart and find your connection.

You must know for which harbor you are headed if you are to catch the right wind to take you there. • LUCIUS ANNAEUS SENECA

Inspiration acts as encouragement and is a great blessing. Once you feel encouraged, there should be no problem going ahead with any kind of practice. Obstacles here and there won't stop you, because you are going to be a hero. You are a hero already. Why? Because you have become a strong, powerful person, full of encouragement, because you are inspired.

A wonderful way to do this is through meditation, and I will show you how to get started. I am very happy to discover that Western people are very fond of meditation, which I consider excellent for spiritual practice. Meditation gives us insight and it gives us wisdom, which is the antidote to ego. The insight that comes through meditation, with practice, can be totally free from the usual fabrications with which we view ourselves and our lives. We can begin to let go of all the conditions we usually place on our words or actions, realizing that action is the thing, not the result.

It's the action, not the fruit of the action, that's important. You have to do the right thing. It may not be in your power, may not be in your time, that there'll be any fruit. But that doesn't mean

you stop doing the right thing. You may never know what results
from your action. But if you do nothing, there will be no result.
• MAHATMA GANDHI

There are two types of meditation: the analytical meditation that requires you to use your brain to understand the basic nature of the world, and sitting meditation that requires you to leave your mind in a peaceful state by being there in the present, without analyzing yourself. Just be aware of yourself, and try not to get lost.

Meditation helps us to calm down, ease our wandering thoughts and simply sit still. Then, we can begin to investigate and find our own path. We have lots of different ways to get to the path, but they all lead to one direction. So don't worry what "level" you are at; just practice, and time will tell you—you don't really have to worry where you are.

There is formal and informal meditation. I think when beginning, the informal meditation is more beneficial and even more meaningful. With formal meditation, we are supposed to think of "nothing," but to be honest, that is extremely hard. We may sit in silence, but in reality spend a lot of time pretending to be meditating, and we tend to lose ourselves. We don't really know what is happening around us; our minds are a bit lost, wandering all over the place.

With informal meditation, we listen to ideas and then spend time in contemplation. For example, we look at the sun rising and think about impermanence and the power of the present, or we look at people as we contemplate how we are all in the same boat, how all people are really the same. This type of meditation is in fact familiarization—familiarizing yourself with the things around you, doing it now, right at this moment, even as you make a cup of tea first thing in the quiet of the morning. It is very helpful for us to check ourselves, investigate our faults, and try to minimize them by developing good qualities and good motivations.

It is good to be alone in a garden at dawn or dark, so that all its shy presences may haunt you and possess you in a reverie of suspended thought. • JAMES DOUGLAS

Everything can be a meditation. We can start to analyze compassion, devotion, true love and the like. We can even meditate in a very informal way in our daily lives—at work, for example. At these times, we can check in with ourselves as situations arise, noting how we react and what lessons we learned. We can find everyday illustrations for such concepts as compassion and attachments. Once we see the true relevance of these things within our own day-to-day lives, they will become so much richer and closer to us, rather than some strange teaching that is all very well but does not relate to the real world.

Often we get caught up in our own desires, not caring about what's happening around us. As we begin to notice the details of the world, then we will discover things and people that move us, inspire us. It doesn't have to be a big thing, but something that really catches your attention. Every movement, every thought and every appearance can be taken as a true teaching. This kind of everyday teaching is a hundred or maybe a thousand times better than formal teaching, especially to accelerate our knowledge and development. Wherever possible, it is much better, I think, to find teachings from what is happening around us.

Begin this practice by simply familiarizing yourself with the things around you. Perhaps you will set aside a little time to do this, and then gradually bring the practice with you into your day. Say you sit on the train with your head buried in a boring newspaper, because that's just what you do. Try taking in the details instead, all those interesting people or views you have never noticed before. Ah, and there's an elderly woman who would hugely appreciate a sit-down, and thanks you for being so kind when you offer your seat; if you'd been reading your paper as usual, you wouldn't have even noticed her.

For me, contemplation helps me to really relax. It is like swimming in a deep ocean. I have peace of mind, which is very much a blessing and shows that the aspiring mind is functioning. I'm not so much one for bliss in sensual terms, but, through contemplation, I feel a deep understanding that is very peaceful and profound. Just by looking around me, I am then inspired; it happens almost spontaneously.

As you consider the situation around you more, I also encourage you to meditate on your own personal situation that you are going through, your ups and your downs. There is no need for you to keep this secret from yourself and push your feelings down; reveal them to yourself, so you may contemplate them and learn whatever lessons you can. This is often not as easy as it sounds; we have so many layers of ego and misunderstandings about ourselves that it is sometimes easier to cheat ourselves. You have to open your secrets to yourself and really explore them from different angles.

For example, if you are feeling fearful or anxious about some-thing, then don't simply dismiss yourself as being silly, self-absorbed or weak. Contemplate what is behind those feelings, what is at their heart, and then begin to see if you can look at them from a more positive angle. Yes, you are fearful, but if you are fearful of something going wrong then this often means you have in front of you an exciting opportunity to do something meaningful. If you are fearful something may not last, can you bring yourself back into the present and discover your inspiration again, rather than focusing on your fear of loss?

Imagination cures the chaos in the heart. • TIBETAN PROVERB

Meditation and contemplation are very helpful for breaking negative cycles; using your aspiring mind, you may see a situation from a new angle, or find a lesson in the challenges of the day. If you find yourself saying, "Oh, here I go again," or "Why does this always seem to happen to me?" you can spend a little time giving yourself room to breathe and think more clearly, and perhaps you will see that you needn't follow the same pattern again; you may find new inspiration to take a different path. Through this practice you will begin to let go of the wild, wandering mind and also the distractions we all have, which often take up so much room in our minds. Instead of imagining all the negative what-ifs that may occur from a situation in your life, you will instead be thankful for where you are right now.

I have seen a few texts that speak of compassion and loving kindness and say that one has to be compassionate to oneself. After that, you can begin to practice compassion to others. You need to give yourself a break so that you may have more patience and tolerance. I tend to say *think of others first* in my teachings, as a little reminder of the motivation behind thinking of yourself. That way, we don't get caught up in our egos, and we remember that by taking care of ourselves we will strengthen our true cause, which is to take care of others.

> *Fill your mind with compassion.*
> • BUDDHA

The Rootless Mind

We have to realize the rootless quality of the mind. If we allow the mind to grow roots, then we trap it into always thinking in the same patterns. We tell ourselves we can only be happy under certain conditions: the weather must be nice, not so cold, not so hot, we have had a good meal, we are having fun. And then when the conditions change, our minds become unhappy or even angry. Your personality switches in a moment. You might get hungry, and so your mind gets moody. Earlier in the same day, you were so happy and then it's gone. It's easy to let external conditions rule our minds. Our ego is easily upset. Not only that, but the mind will cling to rigid views and attitudes if we allow it.

And yet, if we can train our minds to be more relaxed, then we develop resilience to external conditions and to impermanence. It doesn't mean we are directionless, but we can go more with the flow. We can recognize that we create a version of reality through perception and interpretation, that things are not fixed, and that others may easily have a different perception from our own. For example, you may think of something as particularly beautiful. For you it is so attractive, but this is not necessarily true for other people. It may be a human being, or it may be a painting or a house. Whatever it is, it is your mind creation, and why should we all think the same? We all create our own reality, and it is very freeing to accept that.

It sounds like a contradiction, but if you can appreciate the rootless, flowing quality of the mind, then you can begin to tame it. It might feel disconcerting to think of the mind as rootless; so often we search for the things in life that ground us, and that includes the way we think. We have our mental personality—the way we tend to judge the world and people around us, our ways of seeing, our filters and lenses. But from a positive point of view, if the mind is rootless, then there is so much potential; it is the ultimate freedom. It is a key to the door of realization, compassion, everything.

With meditation, we tame this rootless mind without chaining it down. So we encourage clarity and focus to come in, while also allowing the mind to flow and be free—free to take you on your path. You may get to see your purpose, what inspires you, more clearly, and also be able to work out how to get there, what you need to do today. It's like a treasure box, and with some understanding about yourself and acceptance for who you are, you can open things up and get to everything inside.

We don't recommend trying to stop or avoid your thoughts while meditating. Yes, thoughts are fabrications, and we want to gradually get to know our inner nature. But it is very hard to avoid thoughts, and so you may end up pretending to have a clear mind when really it is full. We recommend that you allow your thoughts to come, and then to gently let them go. Don't put your attention on them; take note and then let them drift off. Your mind is like a child making a lot of noise; if you let him be in the knowledge he is cared for, then in the end he will calm down by himself. You may need to be patient, and the same is true for your mind, but eventually complaints and demands will quiet down. Thoughts will come but they will go; positive, negative, it does not matter. Let it be but don't pay attention. Slowly your mind will rest in a nonfabricated way; you will have peace of mind.

BEGINNING MEDITATION

1. Having a quiet place and space in which to contemplate the day can be very helpful, especially for beginners. As you practice, external noises and distractions won't affect you so much.

2. Sitting nice and straight opens up your body and encourages a sense of balance.

3. Eyes should be relaxed and gently focused on an object in front of you. The eyes are very sensitive and often directly control your mind. If your eyes are moving around and in motion, then the mind will also be busy and disturbed. So eye posture is important, and if you can look downward slightly, you will find what is most peaceful for you. Often, people think that to meditate you need to close your eyes. But we recommend open-eye meditation, because if you close your eyes, then you might feel temporarily very good with no distractions, but as soon as you open your eyes, you will be disturbed more that usual. Or there will be a contrast between meditating and the real world, when really you want to bring meditation into your daily life—to synchronize your days and nights with the meditative state of mind.

4. To begin your time of contemplation, you may want to start by focusing on the breath and taking it to all areas of your body.

5. For many people, it is a case of "thinking too much." If you find your head is buzzing, with thoughts flitting all over the place and no helpful focus on any one of them, then take this time to really focus on your slow breath. Gradually slow your thoughts down and allow them to drift off, leaving what's really important at the center—something you might then want to concentrate on.

6. As you think about the day, ask yourself if you felt a dominant "grasping" emotion. For example, were you frustrated or angry about anything, were you bored or jealous or greedy? If any of these emotions formed a part of your day, have a look at them now that you are calm and sitting quietly. Turn them over in your head and think about how you might learn from them or transform them into a positive. Look at the details and understand just how impermanent they are too.

7. Go ahead and try for a couple of minutes. We recommend people meditate for short but sharp periods rather than long and dull. Dull meditation leads to bad habits, and so it is better to practice in a sharp, clear way, even if that is just for a very short time to begin with.

Don't be frightened of the stillness. We are surrounded by many
distractions and noises in everyday modern living, so taking even
a few minutes to be quiet and do nothing is often very challenging.
We wear our busyness as a badge of honor, hardly having time to
eat or have a cup of tea, let alone contemplate the day. You may
even feel a little agitated and restless at first, as though you can't
sit still. But even a few minutes sitting up on your comfortable
bed, warm and with no distractions, will be very powerful. Allowing your mind to settle and slow down is the best energy recharge
you can give it. Your clarity of thought will begin to return; focus
will be easier, even as you go through the day. Decisions you found
so difficult or complicated will happen in the blink of an eye as you
get to know yourself and what you really want from life. You will
know how to listen to your heart, and your sense of time will open
up and stretch, no longer hurling by at a frantic pace, but going
along nicely, allowing you to live each moment to the next.

Try to relax and put yourself into a spacious, nonfabricated
state of mind. Give it a little space to rest. Just stay there and see
what it does. I think this is a good start. Stretch your spine, and
relax. Don't try to do anything; just *be* for a little while.

As well as taking a little time out during the day for contemplation, doing physical activities will often quiet the mind and give
you a sense of deep relaxation, afterward if not always during.
Going for a strenuous walk, jogging or working out, especially in
a class or with music, means you put all your effort into your body,
allowing your mind to have a welcome rest and recuperation.
Often, solutions seemingly present themselves to problems that
seemed insurmountable while at the office; the solution was always
there, but it is that you have given your mind a chance to find
clarity by giving it a break from the daily clutter.

The Practical Mind

After developing the inspiration or aspiring mind, you can then work on the practical mind. You can really begin to focus, make decisions and use your mind to give you the strength and commitment to go ahead and act. Your practical mind is also where you nurture your attitudes of generosity, patience, humility, and so on, working on how you will put them into practice.

It's important to develop your inspiration mind first, so that your motivation for practice will be selfless. Without this, you may find your ego often gets in the way. For instance, when practicing generosity, you may give a little and expect something back as a result. Or you may be very disappointed if you are not thanked. You attach conditions to your generosity, you show patience only with the people you like! With a truly inspired mind, your motivation is purely to give, no strings attached.

As you practice, you can use meditation to check in on how you are doing, both mentally and in your day-to-day actions. You can check whether you are progressing or not, whether your wisdom and compassion are developing. You can contemplate your thoughts and experiences, and start to work out if there are situations or people in your life who are either right or wrong for you. You have to look at your experiences through your heart; everything positive and negative is within you—it isn't given to you by others, whatever the appearances are to the contrary.

You are now exercising the part of your mind that will give you a really strong attitude to do good things based on what has inspired you. Like so many things, one without the other is not so good. Just as taking care of yourself without taking care of others is no good, so is taking care of others without taking care of yourself. There are always two sides to a coin. Use your inspiration mind to find your way and make your promise, and then harness the power of your practical mind to act on that promise, to walk your path.

How to Live Alone Mentally

Loneliness is a great fear for many people, and yet the ability to live alone in yourself, independent of others, is a great strength and skill. With this strength, you will be even happier in your relationships, as there will be no chain of dependence, but rather relaxed enjoyment.

Developing your mind through contemplation will develop your ability to be alone, both mentally and physically. Many people find it difficult to sit still for five minutes, let alone explore their thoughts and feelings. But by taking a little refuge or retreat from the busyness of your life, by taking time to sit in the park and watch the butterflies, learning how to be still and attentive, this will bring you a great sense of contented confidence.

Don't force yourself to be alone; take it gently. For some people, even if they take to the mountains on retreat, their minds remain in the city, unable to be alone. So, start small, a few minutes at a time in a place that is peaceful and calming *for you*, whether that is in the park, sitting on the sofa, or up that mountain.

Most people are about as happy as they make up their minds to be. • ABRAHAM LINCOLN

Act with Love and Kindness

Guard well within yourself that treasure, kindness.
Know how to give without hesitation, how to lose
without regret, how to acquire without meanness.

• GEORGE SAND

Many people are afraid to love themselves, believing it to be selfish or indulgent in some way. But to practice compassion for others, you first have to know how to love yourself. I'm not talking about feeding your ego, but to contemplate your life and your motivations and appreciate just how precious life is. Once you know yourself, then you know that everybody else has exactly the same feelings, and this understanding gives you good reason to be compassionate to others. If you understand how to improve your own life, then you know how to take care of others. This is a very creative and positive thing to do; I like to call it devotion. You may become a very nice and devotional person! But if we don't know how to truly love ourselves, we naturally won't know how to love others also.

You, yourself, as much as anybody in the entire universe,
deserve your love and affection.

• BUDDHA

What is love, truly? When we understand and feel love, then life is colorful. It is easy to think of love as something that is more about the ego than the true essence of love. It is easy to interpret love as lust, desire and wanting, but really love is understanding. If you have understanding and compassion toward a person, then you will act to help them or be kind to them, unconditionally and genuinely. All of us know deep down how to recognize love, because we've experienced it before, perhaps not even in this life, but at some point.

Think about a moment of love in your life that was completely unselfish, either shown to you or that you gave to another. Bring that memory up inside you, along with the feelings, the warmth. Opening yourself up to these feelings of unconditional love will, in turn, make you receptive to experiencing more of them in your day-to-day life.

To benefit others, you have to have something to share. So, first of all, you must be happy—then you can share happiness. This is what love is. Love is something to share; the practice of love is to share, to give. And through developing your compassion, you get a tremendous amount of happiness that you can then share! So be smiling, be kind and thoughtful. These need to come from the heart, and the heart has to be happy. If you are happy, you automatically smile and laugh; there is no fooling. You are automatically kind and thoughtful if you are happy. You are sharing your smile; you are sharing your glow.

Compassion

I often think that the word *compassion* sounds very religious in the modern age, but I always like to talk about it, because it is actually a very beautiful thing. Compassion is complete understanding. Compassion is the mother or the father, the essence of enlightenment. The Buddha came out of compassion and loving kindness. If I have compassion, then I will give you what you need as best I can with no conditions. I will not put you in a box. I will let you be free and I won't place expectations upon you.

All beneficial activities come from compassion; it is fundamental. Then on top of that, we can build the notion of love, the notion of kindness, everything. Compassion is how the universe works, how people work, how your friendships work.

To really understand compassion, you must first show all these things to yourself. Throw away the labels you use—I call these *square ideas*. Think about your genuine needs. Nothing is hidden, nothing is secret, everything is transparent. If you can discover what it truly means to be you, then you will be happy in your own skin, happy to be by yourself. That sense of understanding will give you a great happiness and a foundation upon which you can build genuine love and genuine kindness. It will give you a freedom that you can then give to others, one of the best gifts of all.

I was giving a talk, and one of my students asked me, "If I take care of others, who will take care of me?" He was starting to worry about himself. It is an interesting question. But, actually, the best way to take care of you is to take care of others. That's the way it works, but often we find it hard to do this or even accept this approach. We want to take care of ourselves by ourselves. That's how we develop our ego, how we learn to survive—the survival of the fittest. But I don't believe that's the way we really want to be.

Alongside love, feelings of fear and vulnerability are natural. Fear is an ally of the ego, constantly trying to keep the status quo, to keep things nice and tidy and just as they are, rather than opening up to new and unknown possibilities. Vulnerability can actually be a very good thing, if we look at it in that way. It accepts that the future is uncertain; it is very honest, very human. If we can learn over time to embrace our vulnerability, we will be less likely to put up those barriers that prevent true love from getting a look inside. How we define or see love is a part of our self-image. So many people describe themselves in terms of love: "I will never find love," "I always get rejected in the end," "I just want to be loved." These are the patterns of thought that our ego creates to keep us where we are, trapped in our beliefs. Or we find love, and then the fear sets in that we might lose it, or it's not quite perfect. We try to control it, and once you try to control love, it can never be true. Love is freedom; love is taking a chance.

Loving Kindness and Respect

If we can develop mutual respect, then loving kindness will naturally blossom. For me, this is the beauty of spirituality, the bottom line. Right now we are not making it easy on ourselves to nurture respect and kindness. The world is set up in such a way that we are told we must consume everything; for a bit of energy, in the blink of an eye we cut down trees that take many decades, or even centuries, to grow. We raise animals for an ever-increasing appetite for meat, instead of living alongside them, eating a few eggs or drinking a little milk here and there. We have fallen into a pattern of using and abusing one another to get our own way; we really have been taught to be selfish, because we fear it is either that, or we will be left behind while others gather up all the riches.

Meditation and contemplation help us to counteract this attitude and gradually develop our selflessness. I don't think many people truly feel all that comfortable with the way things are; it is not a nice feeling to put yourself ahead at the expense of others, but sometimes it's difficult to know what else to do. As you develop your compassionate mind, you begin to have the confidence to try a different way, and to know that all those times you show respect or act with kindness are worth so much more than striving to be number one, to be the best.

WHAT DOES LOVE MEAN TO YOU?

Allow yourself to explore all your feelings around the word *love*. Some will be happy, some more sad or full of regret. I'm not saying dwell on the unhappiness, but accept it and then allow yourself to move on from these old patterns of feeling. Anything can happen today and tomorrow, so don't label yourself, but perhaps take a few lessons with you and give yourself the chance to heal.

The Buddhist teacher and philosopher Nagarjuna said that compassion is like "water needed for harvesting." It is needed while working in the fields, while the crops are growing, and even when they are grown. In the same way, compassion is very important for a beginner starting on the path, and later, as they progress along the way. Compassion and true love are needed in the beginning, the middle and the end.

Our path in life comes from a cause, and *is* the cause. The key is that it is a compassionate path. Whatever we do and whatever we say has to come out of compassion and love, instead of from our ego or from selfish attitudes. All the ideas I am giving you in this book are given to inspire you to first develop your compassion and then put it into practice. It is as simple, and so very difficult, as that. Because none of the Buddhas have ever been realized without practicing; the path is also the practice. We just need to try, even if we are beginners, to do a little day by day, to practice.

If you want, you can bring harmony, happiness, understanding and enlightenment to the world. Enlightenment may be some distance away, but you can still share your warmth with others; you can become softer through understanding. We know the people we like to be with because it feels warming, nourishing and peaceful. Other people are very cool, so that you feel as though you are even touching something cold. Being with them doesn't make you feel warm—these people don't have the courage to love themselves, so they have nothing to share.

If you are struggling to see a situation or person with compassion, then try looking from a different angle. There's no need to be stuck in your ways; just as no day is the same as yesterday or to-morrow, we can easily change ourselves, our thoughts and our attitudes. It's good to change our minds. It will set you free.

We all have to spend some amount of time in this world. We can choose to make the lives of ourselves and others very miserable, or we can choose to encourage one another. We all know that life sometimes can be very hard and depressed. Therefore to constantly be able to inspire and encourage one another is a great deed, no matter what religions, cultures, nationalities and backgrounds you belong to.

Some people I meet never seem to think they can be this way; they are not "good enough." They compare themselves to others who show great patience or kindness and think, "We aren't great, so how can we be like them. We can't even hope to be like them." Lacking confidence, they are already discouraged.

It is wrong to think we cannot change; we will never be able to develop by putting ourselves down. We cannot learn *everything*, but we have to nurture and encourage ourselves, and why shouldn't we? Why not? This is the attitude we have to have. If there is no hope to be a great person, if the potential for enlightenment is not there, why bother? But we know deep down that we have potential. You have seen glimpses already along the way of your life, felt those moments of real understanding and clarity and true happiness. Now is the time to open those moments up and see that making others happy will make you happy. This also becomes a practice of keeping your own awareness in the present moment; we can adjust and tune ourselves to go with the natural rhythm of the world, of others. We can be with the world harmoniously, because we realize nothing is permanent, everything flows and is changing. This is how you begin to make the path less traveled a little smoother and well trodden.

The Buddhas became Buddhas by taking care of others.

• BODHICITTACHARYAVATARA

Be Generous:
Aid, Inspire and Protect

That best portion of a good man's life,
His little, nameless, unremembered acts of kindness and love.
• WILLIAM WORDSWORTH

Just like happiness, kindness and love, generosity breeds more generosity. It's difficult to say that there can ever be a selfless act of generosity, because giving happiness to others is the best way to give happiness to yourself. But the key with practicing generosity is to do so without *expectation* of anything in return—this is the hard part. So even if you start small and give just a little, that is good, if you can do so from the heart and with no selfish conditions attached. Of course, if somebody thanks you, it is very nice, but if you don't get any thanks, it doesn't matter— you just give anyway.

Generosity isn't just about giving in a material way. If you can teach or inspire another person, that is an excellent practice of generosity; inspiration is one of the greatest gifts. You can also give protection or care to someone—another act of generosity. Patience, tolerance, respect, laughter, appreciation, kindness and compassion are all wonderful gifts that we have to offer every day, when we think about it.

*There is a wonderful mythical law of nature that the three things
we crave most in life—happiness, freedom, and peace of mind—
are always attained by giving them to someone else.*

• PEYTON CONWAY MARCH

*I just arrived back from a very fruitful walking pilgrimage to
Maratika and back. When we were tired, there would always seem
to be someone along the way selling local food and fresh water. I
could not believe that, even in such a remote area, almost everything
was available when we needed it.*

*The funny thing was that, whenever anything was being shared
out, I was always the first one to get it. Sometimes I was given far
too much, as each of the two hundred people walking along with
us tended to want to give me something. I didn't want to disappoint
anyone by refusing their gifts, so I had to carry all these things and
didn't know what to do. But then I discovered a very good method.
I kept the things they gave me for a couple of hours as a show of
my appreciation, and then I gave them back, which made them
happy too. Unfortunately, I discovered this solution a little late, but
now I know what to do next time.*

Some of the great Indian yogis, a thousand years ago, said in
their texts that they have learned how to practice generosity by
first giving things from their right hand to their left, and then from
left to right. They did this very simple thing to train themselves to
give. It almost seems childish, but perhaps that is why it works—
starting very small and gradually getting bigger and bigger. In this
way, when you do give something away—whether something
physical, inspiration or protection—you do so by allowing yourself to give, not forcing yourself at all. You don't feel any regrets

or any need to show off. A good way to start is by dividing what you can give in two, and give half to others, and the other half keep for yourself; you share. In this way, we gradually get back to a sense of pure motivation, with no strings attached or need to tell the world what we have done. The act is enough in itself.

No act of kindness, no matter how small, is ever wasted.
• AESOP

When we make such actions from the heart, it gives us a cooling, peaceful, happy feeling. We Buddhists call this a *shila*. You are not proud, but appreciative. The practice is sincere and genuine— and being sincere gives a tremendous feeling of joy and satisfaction, rather than acting out of a feeling of burden or guilt. Give willingly and with joy in your heart. Even if you have nothing material to give, it does not matter. You just have to open your heart and let go of your burning attachments to things or people. Give others freedom, and you will be free yourself. We all have to be brothers and sisters. You may be rich, I may be poor. It does not matter. Whatever kind of language you speak, it does not matter. Regardless of who you are, we are all the same. We all go through different experiences, but at the end of the day, we each have nothing in our hands. So we cry together, we laugh together, we mourn together, we enjoy together, we help each other.

In many, many lifetimes, Buddha Shakyamuni gave his life and his body. Once, in Nepal, he gave his entire body to a tiger and we can still see the spot where this occurred. The hungry tiger was going to eat her own baby and out of compassion, knowing what was going to happen, he offered his body. Because the tiger was too weak to

*eat, he cut a vein so she could first lick the blood and finally she
devoured him.*

Most of us are always concerned about making ourselves happy,
doing all sorts of silly and selfish things, without realizing that,
actually, by making others happy, we will be too. You can check
by yourself whether this is true or not. What I am trying to say is,
if you have a big heart that is willing to share your virtues, then
your virtues will actually multiply. The more giving your heart is,
the more you are able to receive. If we give and help without any
expectation or any condition, that itself is a great practice and a
great joy that cannot be measured by any mundane means. In fact,
I can even say that when you help, give or do anything unconditionally that is beneficial, whatever you get in return is also unconditional. It's a pretty fair deal, isn't it? So, say good-bye to any
grasping or selfish attitudes for now, or for the time being, at least.
Ask them to leave you alone.

Presence Is a Gift

If you go through your day with awareness and attention, then you
are really present, and this is a gift too. Everything you do can be
done with a thought to others, even something as simple as enter-
ing a room or having a conversation. You will think of the others
in the room, how you might connect with them, how nice it is to
see them. You listen attentively rather than only thinking about
what you want to say next. You want to share the things that inspire
you, pass on knowledge and encouragement, give what you can.

So finding your purpose and walking your path becomes generous in itself.

I encourage you to dedicate everything for others. If you can manage to do this very gently and very genuinely, you will be doing a brilliant job. This is the uncommon path, as we usually have the tendency to put "myself" at the front. But if you can abandon your own agenda, or start by putting it aside for a little while, then you will benefit many people and in turn develop your own understanding of life a great deal. You will be showered with the benefits.

As this all comes from practice, don't set yourself or your aspiring mind impossible tasks; take it step-by-step. I encourage you to look very gently at yourself and how you are feeling, rather than try to immediately give all your love to the world. Often in the name of love, we end up developing a bigger instead of smaller ego. Our motivation is to make ourselves feel good, rather than to help others. Helping others definitely makes us feel happier in ourselves, but, like the chicken and the egg, it's a question of what comes first—what is your primary motivation. So don't rush headlong into giving away all your worldly goods. Gradually you will work out what you truly want to give to the world and to others. Do whatever you can do completely and without forcing yourself in any way. Take it gently and slowly and begin with appreciation.

But I encourage you to make a start, to act now. People can spend a great deal of time worrying about what is the right thing to do, the best way to help. I say, listen to your heart and then go ahead and *do something*, whatever you can. Just think, your little drop of money, kindness or inspiration goes into a big ocean and will help to contribute to many things out there in the world. You have lots of chances, lots of ways to help others. Even if you do a little thing, dedicate it to everybody, and it will grow in size profoundly. Giving is giving; don't expect anything, but use your own eyes carefully. Then you can trust it will go through good sources to a good cause. I always say that being generous with a big heart makes you gain more than you can ever imagine. It adds meaning and great value to life.

Show Humility and Patience

No longer seeking to consider
What is right and what is wrong.

• BUDDHA

As you practice loosening and letting go of those attachments you have—for example, being too attached to material possessions, to people, your emotions or your view of the world—then you will begin to replace pride with humility. If you are still attached to your body, your looks, youth, wealth or anything, there's no way you can be humble. Letting go will open up your mind and your heart to the wonderful lessons life has to offer you. It will take you off the defensive, because you will begin to see that these lessons are never designed to hurt or humiliate you, to make you feel embarrassed. If you can accept yourself for who you are, then every moment in life becomes an opportunity, or simply an experience along the way.

Pride is always boasting, always talking so it's impossible to hear what anyone else is saying. Pride makes us think we are the knowledgeable one, the intelligent one, the better one. Pride makes you closed so that you lose the chance to receive. But with humility, whatever you want to know, whatever people say, you listen and accept it; in this way, you develop much faster than someone with pride.

It wasn't until quite late in life that I discovered how easy it is to say "I don't know!" • SOMERSET MAUGHAM

You do not need to be proud of your skills or your achievements. This doesn't in any way mean they aren't important, but, rather than defining who you are, they become tools with which you can do your best work. For example, your skill might be with computers. You might be better than good—you might be an expert, but you shouldn't be proud. Perhaps you are a terrible singer, and when it comes time to sing, you can't exactly boast that you are a computer whiz. It's good to laugh about this; so what if we're useless at some things? It's good to know there are times when we are experts, and times when we are nobodies; we're all the same in this respect. And with this understanding, pride soon goes down.

For many people, being useless at things is a source of great discouragement. But I think that is because our pride is getting in the way, our ego is hurt, and this either makes us rather brittle and defensive about our weaknesses, or makes us feel we are useless as a person. So, if we can release our attachments to all these things we do, then it no longer matters if we are great experts or not. We realize it's a good idea to make the most of our talents for the benefit of everyone, but it's no longer necessary to feel bad at all about things we may be less good at. We don't need to take these things to heart. Let them flow away with the stream.

Patience

The practice of patience is the main door to enlightenment. Patience creates space to think and room to breathe. In an argument, patience creates a gap so that you may find a compromise or acceptance. Things just look a whole lot better when you view them with patience. On the other hand, if you don't give yourself a chance to breathe and think, then your own desires will take over and anger will often burst forth! Constantly getting angry or irritated is a difficult way to live.

Adopt the pace of nature: her secret is patience.

• RALPH WALDO EMERSON

If you have patience and tolerance your life will be rich, but they are not instantly easy concepts. That is why so often life is wobbly, like an old antique table. I used to have a very old British dining table, and whenever you went near it, it wobbled and creaked; you couldn't rest anything on it for fear it would break. This is like life without patience and tolerance. They create a very supportive foundation. Whatever happens—and anything can happen in this life—you don't mind; you can cope and you never lose your courage, even when you face pain from others.

Patience helps us in times of suffering; if we have patience, then we will never give up or be discouraged. We persevere and continue to think and do good things. We are able to think of others who are in the same situation as us; we send out our compassion to them, in the hope that they will not have to suffer as we do.

Patience is also extremely helpful whenever we are happy. It is easy to get carried away. You may be full of pride or find you are never quite satisfied and looking for more. If you are the richest in the village, you feel very proud of yourself and look down on others. If you are beautiful and proud of your beauty, you will suffer a lot when you find a pimple or wrinkle on your face. You may be easily jealous of others who are doing better than you. It is good to be happy, healthy—even wealthy. But with patience, you will dispel your pride and realize how impermanent it all is. You will thank your good karma, rather than looking down on others.

The greatest patience is humility.
The greatest meditation is a mind that lets go.
The greatest wisdom is seeing through appearances.
• ATISHA

In the beginning, practicing patience is not easy, but there are many ways to start. Patience and tolerance require a great deal of thought and understanding. It's not easy to be tolerant in the face of things that go acutely against our own morals—what we believe to be right versus wrong, good versus bad. When people may behave, in your view, wrongly, then you cannot take it, because it doesn't fit in with your view of the world. You want everything and everyone to fit in with you, while you also want to be left alone to be yourself. Generally speaking, I would say we are very stubborn. We are not easily influenced by these teachings, or even by what is happening in our lives every day. But remember, all of us, every single one of us, is in the same boat. Do we have much reason to be arrogant or egoistic? After all, who knows what will happen in the next minute? Anything can.

This isn't a message about giving up, about doing nothing while someone keeps on abusing you and being nasty. The message is that with patience in yourself, you become more developed without giving up, without losing courage. You no longer let these things totally overcome and control you. You stop asking "why me?" You stop asking what additional suffering will come tomorrow, and instead ask yourself what you are going to do, how you are going to develop. It is not easy, but if you start with compassion, then you will begin to see.

For example, if someone is very nasty to you, there must be a reason. You should look to have some knowledge and understanding of this person and why he or she gets so irritated. Maybe he is very weak, maybe he doesn't understand you, or perhaps you did something to upset him. If you can understand the cause, then you can defuse those burning emotions you feel. Even if he is acting very badly and all you can do is walk away, you don't need to be attached to the situation; you don't need to carry it with you.

You have to be honest with yourself. When others speak ill of you, if what is said is not true and is merely malicious or ignorant gossip, you don't have to feel pity for yourself—let go and move on. If what is said has some truth to it, you can reflect, correct and look to make improvements. After that, let go of any regretful feeling. Learning to leave things behind is one of the best practices to develop patience and, in turn, compassion and wisdom.

At the bottom of patience is Heaven.
• TIBETAN PROVERB

Contemplation Develops Patience

As you spend time contemplating your day-to-day life, you will begin to think about how you deal with things. You can learn from your experiences and think about how you might be in similar situations in the future. Thinking things through in your head will help to shine a light and slow things down, creating that space you need in which to gradually develop your patience.

It is also very helpful if you can bring these thoughts down into your heart and see how you really feel. A person you know well or a complete stranger may have truly annoyed you today, and you felt you couldn't help but snap. At the time, you felt they really deserved to know just how angry you were with their actions, their words or their selfish attitude. But perhaps letting out that anger didn't feel so good after all, and so you contemplate how you might approach a similar situation if one should arise. You don't want to be passive, a pushover, but you want to get your message across calmly and with strength.

As you develop your patience, people may call you a very understanding person. By this I mean a person who understands the situation around him or her. You can take it all in quite easily, smoothly and gently, without making a big fuss out of small things or raising your voice high up to the sky—in other words, without being short-tempered, which is just a lack of practice. Through contemplation and meditation, it is possible to stretch the temper so it can become as long as a mile. This type of meditation is familiarization—becoming intimately familiar with your experiences and your feelings, and those of others. Today, maybe, you find this difficult, but gradually, if you keep practicing, after only a week or two, you will definitely be a bit better. After a month or two, patience will come more easily, and next year you will be a chief negotiator.

Practice Develops Patience

One of the great masters in Tibet had many disciples, and one day a disciple came to him and asked to be accepted. The master asked, "Yes, of course, but do you have any qualifications?" and the disciple answered, "No, I have none." The master asked him many questions, but every time he answered that he had nothing, he just wanted to be a disciple. Eventually he felt he had to say something, so he told the master, "I have a reputation of being a person without anger. That's all I have." "Oh," said the master, "that's the greatest qualification you can have. Please join us to hear my teachings."

At the next gathering, the master said, "Until today, we have had such a nice time here, without any problems, but from now on we have to be very careful. There is a thief in our group. Though none of us has much to steal, we may still have a little bit to eat and a few things to wear. We don't want them stolen, so we must be watchful, because one of us is a thief and that's him over there." The master pointed to the man who said he had no anger. He was so embarrassed and felt terrible, started sweating, but couldn't say anything in front of the great master.

This went on for several months. The master would say in front of thousands of disciples, "Did you lose anything? Oh, good, because he is such a thief. I worry night and day about all of you."

Finally, after a very long time, the disciple became very angry. He could no longer control himself. "Who said I'm a thief?" he screamed in front of everyone. The master looked at him. "Didn't you say that you never got angry? I thought you didn't have any anger, but really, you do, don't you?" In that way, the disciple was able to realize that anger was there, and it was very much an awak-

ening, a great lesson given with love, as he went on to become a
great disciple.

It isn't easy to practice patience when you are feeling calm and
at one with the world. Even as you read my words telling you how
important patience is, I can't help you nearly as much as your trying it out in the real world. So if someone comes and provokes
your anger, does something nasty to you, that person is the real
master. Of course, in the moment, we don't realize that and feel
that they are an enemy. But they are giving you a real chance to get
into the practice, so grab it whenever you can.

Keep Walking

Your work is to discover your work
And then with all your heart
To give yourself to it.

• BUDDHA

A great violinist brings so much joy to the world through her playing, but to do that she must practice over and over; she must have great diligence. If she does so with joy in her own heart, then she has found her true cause, her true path. If she does this with a heavy heart, loaded down with expectations, then she cannot give her music unconditionally. Life is difficult if your heart's not in it. But once you do find the thing you want to do, whether that is to be more patient or learn new skills so that you may help people in some way, what you have to do next is practice. You have to keep walking.

Once you have developed your inspirational mind, you open yourself up to finding your purpose. And if you can make a vow, a promise, to yourself to follow your path, then you will create a beautiful foundation upon which to practice. If you are going in the direction that moves you, that gives you great happiness, then you will be happy to practice hard, because you will feel like yourself, immersed and in the stream of your life. This brings genuine satisfaction and contentment; it is a tremendous sense of relief to get completely involved with what you are meant to do.

The reason why most of us have difficulty receiving the blessing of things such as health and wealth, without the help of somebody else—without praise, for example—is that we lack the confidence that comes with this sense of devotion, of complete involvement. We miss the importance of taking care of the foundation, the roots, and are distracted by always looking after the flowers, the fruit and the things at the top of the tree. But if we don't take care of the roots, over time there will be less and less fruit to harvest.

Discipline and Diligence

In the modern world, many people are not really sure if discipline or diligence are such good things. They make people feel as though they have to act in a certain way, that they are being controlled in some way, penning themselves in, rather than living as freely as they choose. Since it is so difficult to practice discipline by ourselves without any help, Buddha and other divine beings like Jesus Christ were forced to say something—to give constitutions and tell you what you should and should not do. These are helpful, but sometimes feel like a kind of burden. You want to drink something, but cannot do so according to the teaching. Whatever you want to eat, it seems that it is not allowed. This is why it is so freeing to develop the aspiring mind, as you then begin to know spontaneously what discipline is, rather than having to be told. You will live with love and compassion straight from the heart, which is so much more enjoyable.

We can embrace diligence by viewing it from a slightly different angle, one that reminds us that it is with discipline that the
truly wonderful musicians practice so that they may give us such
listening pleasure and relaxation. If we engage discipline within
ourselves, then we are able to train our minds so that we can calm
our wandering thoughts, even while surrounded by the busyness of
modern living. Diligence is really a form of devotion, and devotion
is a form of understanding. With diligence and devotion, we stick
to our good commitments rather than saying we'll start tomorrow, and if we have found our inspiration, then we will be fortunate enough to enjoy our hard work. I always say that intelligence
means nothing without diligence.

> The great Indian master Asanga was practicing on Maitreya. It's a
> long story, but to make it short, after practicing for three years, he
> hadn't gained anything. As he came down from his retreat, he saw
> a man rubbing a big iron rod with a piece of cotton. Seeing how
> hard he was working, Asanga asked what the man was doing. "I
> want to make a needle out of this iron rod to sew my clothes."
> Asanga realized that all the practice he had been doing for the past
> three years up on the mountain was nothing compared with what
> this man was doing, just for a needle!
>
> So Asanga returned to his retreat for three more years, but again
> failed to achieve anything. He felt very discouraged and almost
> decided he should just give up; he was never going to realize any-
> thing. Leaving his cave, he saw a man brushing the mountain with
> a feather and asked him why. "My house is down below and, because
> of this mountain, I get very little sunshine," the man replied. "I'm
> trying to make the mountain smaller so that I may get a little more

sun."Asanga thought, if this man was prepared to do that for the sake of a little extra sunshine, the least he could do was return to his retreat and practice some more.

Many years passed in this way. Every three years, Asanga saw something that confirmed the importance of diligence. After twelve years, he left his retreat and while on the road saw a dog in great pain. The lower part of its body was rotten, filled with insects and germs, but the upper part was still OK. Seeing the dog, he felt a great compassion and felt he should try to do something to help get rid of the insects and germs. But if he touched them with his hands they would die, so he closed his eyes and used his tongue to clean the dog, which was softer than his hands and so wouldn't kill the insects. As he did this, the dog disappeared, and when he looked up Maitreya was sitting on the rock in front of him. Asanga cried, "Where have you been all this time? I practiced for twelve years and you never came." Maitreya replied, "I was there many times, but you were not diligent enough. Each time you came out of the cave I was there to help you. The dog was also me. I appeared to ripen your compassion before you could then prove your diligence."

Then Asanga flew with Maitreya to his pure land where he received many teachings. When he later returned to earth, he wrote many books on what Maitreya taught him. We are still studying those books today.

If you break your promise, if you give up, then don't feel bad, but renew it as soon as possible without delaying even a night. Don't feel disheartened or that you aren't good enough somehow to carry on. It is easy to be too humble when it comes to practicing, but you can restore your discipline happily and quickly. Otherwise, negativities will tend to grow and soon accelerate. Whatever we decide we want to do, we really need to nourish that promise to ourselves. Just like a plant, it needs to be watered and fed and looked after nicely so it can grow. You need to take care of your promises, your sense of purpose, willingly and happily rather than under any kind of duress. If you are forcing yourself, then perhaps you need to look back at your inspiration and rediscover your motivation, as feeling that we *have* to do things just becomes a burden that weighs and slows us down, making us little good to anybody. We may get through life OK fulfilling our obligations, but it isn't nice, and by opening up your heart and mind you will discover there is another way.

The Cooling Balm of Discipline

Discipline can bring us great comfort. If you feel out of control in a situation and literally hotheaded, then discipline acts like a cooling balm, like a fan that eases the burning emotions that have sprung up, and helps to relax you. This kind of inner discipline is the best, as it comes from your nature. It takes time to develop, which is why religions and traditions like Buddhism have many teachings and practices to help create this sense of control. But practicing as you walk the uncommon path is very helpful for dealing with afflictive emotions such as anger, jealousy and desire. Your path is your refuge, where you feel comfortable, relaxed and calm. The path takes you to a state of mind that dispels misunderstanding. We can come across both very beautiful things and very bad, ugly things and not be carried away.

To be in control is actually a very freeing thing when that control comes from a place of love and compassion, both for yourself and for others. Being controlling when you are not happy about yourself or you are judging others as not being good enough is the opposite; this creates invisible chains that bind you to very particular ways of doing things. You have become a slave to your burning emotions and blinkered in the way you see yourself and the world. But inner control that allows you to listen while others speak, to value all human beings rather than jump to conclusions, and to practice being your true self rather than try to live up to or run away from the labels you have grown up with, is deeply relaxing and frees your mind to consider the important things in life.

As you develop this inner, relaxed discipline, you will feel peaceful and happy—not proud, but appreciative. It also brings sincerity. Being sincere and genuine about any kind of practice will give you a tremendous feeling of satisfaction and joy from what you are doing, and you will feel that you are very lucky. You won't need to show off to anyone else about your discipline, but quietly you will be thankful for it.

Even a small community like Druk Amitabha Mountain is nourished by different people with individual skills. But the most important, I think, is having people with heart, not only skills. What's the point of skills without the heart to help or the sense of responsibility to make sure that things are finished properly? There is no point in having skills without heart; nothing works that way. I really feel that, in everything you do, you must do it with a sincere and full heart to accomplish things nicely and with inspiration for what you are doing. Isn't that the best way to use your knowledge and your talents?

Having patience I should develop enthusiasm;
For Awakening will dwell only in those who exert themselves.
Just as there is no movement without wind,
So merit does not occur without enthusiasm.
What is enthusiasm?
It is finding joy in what is wholesome.
Its opposing factors are explained as laziness,
attraction to what is bad
And despising oneself out of despondency.
Because of attachment to the pleasurable taste of idleness,
Because of craving for sleep
And because of having no disillusion with the misery of samsara,
Laziness grows very strong.
Just as I would swiftly stand up if a snake came into my lap,
Likewise if any sleep or laziness occur, I shall quickly turn them
back.

▪ SHANTIDEVA, BODHISATTVACHARYAVATARA

PART THREE

Overcoming Obstacles Along Your Way

The one who masters the gray everyday is a hero.

• FYODOR DOSTOYEVSKY

Life is really the greatest teacher of these lessons. Often it seems as though life wants to throw down many obstacles in our way, but sometimes it is a case of how we look at life; are we looking for problems or solutions?

If you can bring some of the thoughts that you have had reading this book into your day-to-day life, that is a gift to those around you and to yourself. Do you find you have a great deal of stress in your life? Or are you short-tempered? Perhaps you lack confidence in your relationships, whether as a partner or a parent. Or you know that fear is in some way holding you back from walking your path. There are chapters in this final section that I hope may help to unblock you, so that you may see things from a different angle. Don't blame anybody else when you are struggling with obstacles; just realize what you are going through.

Everyday life is life. To feel more comfortable with the world and in yourself, to have inner freedom, is not something you need to go and be in a cave to find out about. It is right here, in your every moment. How can you make today a better source for tomorrow?

How to Deal with Stress

All the suffering in the world comes from thinking of oneself.
All the Happiness in the world comes from thinking of others.

• SHANTIDEVA

Stress is one of the main problems in our life; it is very common and an important issue to talk about. It is one of the biggest distractions, and so we need to understand our relationship with it, to find out its cause, why we are all so caught up in "busy-for-nothingness" and misunderstanding.

My friends tell me how much stress they are going through because of the economy, business, family and all sorts of things. Out of curiosity, I checked the dictionary for the modern scholars' explanation of stress and found this definition: "Stress is the consequence of the failure to adapt to change." I think, to a certain extent, they are right about this.

Stress is a result of inflexibility and nonacceptance. In other words, it is caused by strong attachments to certain things, certain ways or outcomes, to expectations. When there is strong hope or expectation, there is also fear that this expectation will not come true, that things may not go according to your plan or your wishes. So stress comes.

Today, most of the people who come and see me tell me that they are easily burned out and that they cannot rest in peace. Our minds become like wild elephants, constantly spinning with thoughts, ideas, and deadline after deadline. So even if our physical activities are not that active, we are still overthinking and giving ourselves useless stress. Even in our dreams we can feel it. Most of the time, we kill our own possibilities by being restless. I think to a certain extent, restlessness is the direct opposite of confidence. That is why we begin to feel so unwell and stressed when we realize that our life is literally carrying us away, and we don't know how to stop it or even slow things down.

Thinking of this upsets me. One of my friends was almost crying because, despite all his success in business, he felt very stressed trying to maintain his success. Even though he had made a lot of money, he now has to work all hours of the day to keep that level of wealth. I guess when he first started with his business, he must have thought, "Well, if I make a million I will be very happy and contented," but now that he has reached his target, he has given himself another excuse to be stressed out by setting an even higher target. So there is no peace in his mind and no stress-free moment in which he can relax. And so he comes to me with tears in his eyes, not knowing what to do to release the pressure.

The same happens to people in relationships. An old friend told me that when she got married a few years before, she thought her prayers were answered, but now she and her husband are separating because they can no longer stand each other. The thing is that both of these friends were looking externally for their solutions to happiness, whether in money or a good partner. That is why I talk so much of acceptance and of letting go of all these expectations, of appreciating what is right here, right now. If you keep looking outside for a solution, you will never be rid of stress, but if you are grounded and walking with understanding and acceptance of who you are, you will master the skills of living in the present and leave stress by the side of the path.

While others miserably pledge themselves to the insatiable pursuit of ambition and brief power, I will be stretched out in the shade singing. • FRAY LUIS DE LEON

What Am I Doing with My Life?

If you are able to recognize these feelings or can help another person recognize them, then you have a great opportunity to take this as a sign to change things, to have the courage to take time out to slow things down and to contemplate your life. All of us, myself included, should always take some time to be turtles. Take the train and slow yourself down. Give yourself time. We will have clearer vision; we will be able to see life's details with a sense of gratitude. Even if we are facing a lot of difficulties externally, we will not be affected because, due to our understanding, we can appreciate even the difficulties or obstacles we are facing. Don't you agree that whenever we slow down, we see things more clearly?

When my friends stop their daily practice and I ask them why, they tell me it is because they don't have time. Some of them even tell me I can't understand, I'm not in business so I wouldn't know what stress is. I laugh to myself when I hear this; if they knew how many people I have responsibility for, how many children I am feeding, and how many monasteries I take care of, they would know just how much I do understand. I remember when I was thinking about setting up schools for nuns, one in Ladakh and one in Nepal, I worried a great deal. I sat there all day, worrying and calculating. At the end of the day, I realized I had done nothing all day except worry. Nothing was achieved and a day was wasted.

Being stressed is a waste of time, and it kills our creativity and potential. Instead of spending all that time worrying, I encourage my friends to get back into their daily practice. When you feel stressed, you often feel stuck and indecisive, so a little time spent meditating and relaxing is of great benefit. You remind yourself of the meaning of impermanence, the preciousness of life. Even if external situations are going wrong, you can still be fearless and have the courage to be OK, to live a fruitful life and be flexible. You can be genuinely happy, because this happiness comes from within and doesn't depend on the circumstances around you to be a certain, fixed way.

I always hope that my friends and students will pick up their path and practices again; it is the backbone of life and happiness. Without this understanding, it is easy to be overwhelmed by the ups and downs of life, but with this grounding we have the confidence to keep walking rather than get caught up in debilitating feelings.

Stress Is Caused by Conformity

If we live our lives always sticking to some kind of conservative rhythm involving customs, tradition and culture, or our own impossibly high standard, it makes us stressed because we are constantly conforming. If we don't conform, we feel we will get into trouble, we will be labeled a troublemaker. We get a lot of head-aches this way!

Of course, we need some structure. Even in Buddhist teaching, there is structure and form to help us along the way, something to lean on. But we also believe in encouraging people to free the structures *within* themselves to reduce stress and misunderstanding. When we try to be or act a certain way all of the time, this makes us feel very nervous. You may cover it up well and appear fine on the outside, but inside you feel as if you are in knots, or that you are trapped. This is because you have a rigid structure inside; we put ourselves in a kind of box, and then suffer from a lot of stress always trying to live up to our own rules and standards. We think that things, other people, or even we ourselves have to be a certain way, and if they are not quite right, we become agitated. We are too attached to an idea of perfection, fed by our hopes and fears; after all, how can anything in the world be perfect? It is totally subjective. Nothing is perfect, and nothing is wrong. We should just try our best.

Let go of winning and losing
And find joy.
• BUDDHA

What Is "the Best"?

I don't like to say negative things about the modern world in which we live. However, I do see that much of the stress experienced is related to the way in which people are educated, which places such

emphasis on competition. You have to compete with somebody
else to even think you exist, and you have to *be the best*. As no one
can be the best for very long, or perhaps even at all, this causes
many problems. People are constantly looking for the impossible,
causing much stress and worry.

Take business as an example. You may make a million, and then
even a billion, but you will still see a lot of people richer than you.
You will be nobody in front of these guys! You ask yourself what
you have gained, but then compare yourself to those with more,
so you get upset or feel that something is missing. You try to work
harder, no matter whether you can or not. You have to compete,
to run after the rainbow; it is so beautiful, you have to try and
catch it, but of course you cannot.

What is this life if, full of care,
We have no time to stand and stare . . .
• WILLIAM HENRY DAVIES

You may worry that if you slow things down and listen to your
heart, you may have less, that you may not be able to provide so
much for your family who depend on you. This is a very under-
standable concern that will worry many people. But think about
what kind of person you are when you have a great deal of stress
in your life. Are you kind, generous, patient and loving all of the
time, or more short-tempered, frustrated and generally more ab-
sent, both in body and spirit? Are you distracting yourself with
busyness and attaining or keeping possessions, rather than being
fully attentive in your life and with those closest to you? Yes, we
have to work and earn a living, but this doesn't mean you have to
become a slave to this existence; you don't have to view life as

being only outside the hours of nine to five. A little more simplicity in your life and a little less expectation will give you a great
sense of freedom, which in turn will stretch out time into a much
more relaxed pace. Don't overstretch, don't strive so hard you
can't ever take a breath; finding a balance in life or walking the
middle path is a quiet, deep and rich joy.

Buddhist Teachings Are Like Space

I speak here from my own experiences and from the experiences
of friends and those around me. The spaciousness of Buddhist
teachings can never be put inside a box. We do have traditions of
meditation, therapies, mental exercises and physical exercises, but
these are to help keep ourselves in a state of peace and calm.

To really give yourself space and freedom, first you have to
free yourself from the many misunderstandings and labels you
have about yourself, your relationships, family—everyone! Almost
everything we do is because we believe in things in a certain way.
Sometimes that is all well and good, and our beliefs are nice and
positive. But we are still setting ourselves up by having such a rigid
belief system, because at some point, someone will disappoint us,
or we will disappoint ourselves by not conforming to our own set
of rules and regulations.

We have to learn to be good listeners and be kind to those who
give us different opinions. Many of my colleagues often disagree
with me and my ways; I don't mind—I am very happy to listen to
their views and respect their ways. We cannot be dogmatic if we
wish to live happily in this world, without stress. A happy mind is
a mind that is open and full of space. If our mind is narrow, then

there is no space to even accept ourselves, and this is when the stress comes. People get jealous and struggle over all kinds of silly things. We should not be fixed; we should be flexible and allow room for others.

We must be willing to let go of the life we planned so as to have the life that is waiting for us. • E. M. FORSTER

Remember that *everything* changes and does not exist with any permanence as it appears to be. This is why it is so important to free ourselves from a sense of *attachment* to any hope, desire or even person. It doesn't mean we don't have hopes, desires or relationships, but that we don't try to fix them in one place, as that can only lead to stress. We don't need to abandon everything and go and live in a cave, but we need this understanding of relative truth in our daily lives.

Everything changes from moment to moment, so why spend so much time and energy worrying about what has been or what is to come? This theory is very important in both meditation practices and in living our daily lives in a more lively, peaceful and happy way. It's good to take things easy. Developing this little bit of knowledge will help us a great deal toward that path. Just a small change in your mind will make a tremendous difference to your life.

Listen to the teachings given by nature itself—teachings such as day turning into night, the changing seasons, the breeze, the sound of a waterfall; all of these teach us about how everything in life is relative, nothing is permanent, and so we can begin to let go of those emotions and thoughts that cloud our enjoyment of life and push us down into stress or nervousness. Things don't have to be a certain way. They can just be.

I was busy clearing up my room like nobody's business, not that it wasn't clean, but it is always good to go through your accumulations of the past year and let go of anything you don't need for the forthcoming year and may hold you back. These things, both physical and emotional, may harm your progress along the path in life and keep you from your cause.

So yesterday here on Druk Amitabha Mountain, all were very busy cleaning. I was very happy standing in the middle of them, watching them climbing up to the window like Mount Everest climbers. It took me ages to clean my own bedroom, I had created so much mess over many days, weeks, even months. The moral of this is, like our own daily spiritual practice, we have to continue doing it all the time, every day if we can, every moment. Otherwise, how can we get rid of all the mess we accumulate over time? It's so much easier to clear a little clutter each day than let it build up into a mountain.

Learning to Be Ourselves

Think of how much we copy one another and do things according to what we are told or what our friends are doing. We copy the way other people live, eat, dress, everything. Then, when we compare ourselves, we sometimes think we are better than others, and other times we think we are worse. This kind of life so many people lead is like a roller coaster. We end up with more and more desires and wanting; we spend more and more money to make ourselves feel better. You may carry thousands of internal pictures with which you compare yourself, a "prettier" person, a "more successful" person. You can't win and it is often painful and hurtful.

If we are not copying one another, then we are often judging whether people are good or bad, right or wrong. If, during a conversation, some of my friends say that a person is very bad, I always feel sad about this. Maybe that person is doing bad things, but who knows if he is truly bad?

Of course, you may dress well and want to look nice, as long as you feel that you don't have to compete with others, but just be yourself. Be happy, no matter whether somebody else is taller, or looking better or worse than you. You just go to your meeting or your party, and come back happy because life is within yourself. There is no jealousy, and you can share genuine positive feelings with others. This is what the modern age needs.

As usual, new people were here to take refuge. The people were standing up, clapping and chitchatting with each other as each person came to take refuge. In Western countries, it is not quite like this; followers tend to be quite serious and get annoyed with anyone who makes even a small noise during these ceremonies. But today everything became quite chaotic; it was difficult to bring everyone into a peaceful mood. But that was also good; seeing them happy and enjoying themselves made me happy too.

Remember that our experiences in life are just that, experiences. They are not us and do not reflect us. Don't cling to your mistakes or criticism. Have the courage to accept them, learn, and then pick yourself up to move on. Day-to-day life should be taken very easily. I know—easier said than done, but think how much more productive you are when truly relaxed, versus when you are consumed by doubts or questions.

Relationships

The freedom you give to others you give to yourself.
• THE GYALWANG DRUKPA

believe that human relationships, especially the positive ones, should grow and become deeper and more genuine as time goes by. This is a great support for one's own life. One hopes that a partner is there to boost one's understanding and spirituality and to make life more colorful, so it is important to choose carefully. Equally, you might find the right partner because you are living a rich and colorful life; as with so many things, perhaps we will never know for sure what comes first.

We should nurture and keep positive and warm relationships with other human beings, with other living beings, trees, flowers— everything in this universe. Genuine spiritual life can be very lonely if you don't have support from friends and beings who are there constantly to keep you on track. But this kind of support is a reciprocal relationship; sometimes you reach out first, and sometimes others reach out to you. As I always say, we don't live in this world or in this universe alone, by ourselves; we are connected with each other. Even if you are the most powerful person on this earth, what does that power matter without any love or support?

Just as we do when looking for happiness, we often put our focus within our relationships in the wrong places. We dwell on the misunderstandings and forget all the things that we have in common and love about each other. This happens a great deal between long-term companions and also between parents and children. "You just don't understand me" is thrown out there, while all the times when we have shown love and compassion are often forgotten. Doubts are the number one killer of our motivation and intention to be a good being, and the number one killer of our relationships with others.

But, just as you can find the happiness within you, you can find the love. And happily, the steps are the same; the first step is to take a bit of time to remember, acknowledge and appreciate all the good things. Once you regain that sense of appreciation, you can begin to look at the hurts in a more constructive and healing way, without bitterness and anger. You can get back to the basics and shine a light on anything positive, then gently talk about things that need resolving or that just need a bit of airing and letting go.

What a happy and holy fashion it is that those who love one another should rest on the same pillow. • NATHANIEL HAWTHORNE

Gratitude within relationships gives them a warm glow. And just as the way to bring happiness into your life is to bring happiness to others, if you can give a partner what they truly need, rather than simply what *you want* to give them, their gratitude will repay you in their smile and their easiness, making your life easy too.

Ask yourself what your partner, your friend, even your boss at work really needs. If they are thirsty, don't show your love with flowers; give them water. If they are tired, let them sleep. This comes from genuine, unconditional understanding, from listening and putting your own needs and desires aside, because as you give others what they need, so too will they often give you what you need. It's not about being controlled by others, which is how so many relationships now exist. Look beneath any surface layers of control to what a person truly needs, which is basically love and compassion, and fulfill that need. Give that person freedom and you will become free yourself.

> *If only I could throw away the urge to trace my patterns in your heart, I could really see you.*
> • DAVID BRANDON, *ZEN IN THE ART OF HELPING*

For example, if I have a partner that I live with, I should understand him or her so that we can live together harmoniously. If we do not understand each other, it will be very hard to live together nicely and comfortably. Our genuine love will be clouded by misunderstanding, making it difficult to share kindness. We may annoy each other or feel the other is a nuisance. I might call her at midnight when she is sleeping soundly to say, "How are you?" I think I'm being kind and making sure she is OK, but she is snoring happily and really doesn't need to be bothered. I should leave her in peace. If I can put myself in her shoes and build understanding, then on top of that we can build love, generosity and a very nice relationship, because if I have understanding, then automatically I will *act* with kindness.

If we understand each other, there is no reason to get so emotional when you are a little bit nasty to me. I won't *mind*. I will be aware of it, but it won't affect who I am and, likewise, I will realize it isn't really who you are either. In this way, we can take situations more easily, smoothly. Even if something terrible or extremely challenging happens, we will be more resilient, less attached, because we have an understanding that our minds shape how we view "reality"—how we view everything and each other.

> He who binds to himself a Joy,
> Does the winged life destroy;
> He who kisses the Joy as it flies,
> Lives in Eternity's sunrise.
> • WILLIAM BLAKE, "ETERNITY"

I call this a kind of smart selfishness, because once you have this understanding, it makes life so much easier. It is common sense, but so easily forgotten: if you want to live very comfortably with your wife, first you have to make her happy, and then she will smile and be very loving to you. If you don't, life will be full of disagreement and stress.

And if we see this relationship with our partner as our first act of kindness, then we can begin to talk about doing the same for our neighbors, our colleagues, our community, even our entire country. It all starts with mutual respect for one another as human beings, and the simple law that if you make others happy, you are bound to be happy too. Yes, we often forget this and end up going in the opposite direction, but if we can be mindful and practice doing our best each day, then you will see the difference you can make.

I'm OK, You're OK

Love, or what we think is love, can often be confused with more burning emotions. It is easy to become very attached to a version of love, but then find that it tends to bring with it emotions like pride, possessiveness, jealousy and insecurity. Our natural, relaxed confidence goes out the window, and we become controlled by our emotions or by our desire to control our partner. Remember, you're OK just as you are, and so is your partner. You're here in this relationship to boost each other, to provide a little support, caring human touch, laughter and, yes, happiness.

You may grow up feeling that you want or need to belong to someone, or that you want someone to belong to you. That to be needed will prove your worth in some way, or that you can feel safe and secure if you depend on your partner. The best way to feel safe and secure is actually to be confident and independent within yourself; that way, you can enjoy your partner's company deeply without either of you being constrained or controlled. You can truly open your heart, because you don't rely on their love; you are just as OK by yourself.

It may take time to develop this confidence if you have always been taught to be dependent, but as you practice some of the ideas in this book, I hope that a feeling of relaxation may grow in you and a sense of independence that enriches your relationships. Right now you may be fearful that you can't be yourself when alone, that your biggest fear in life is indeed to be alone. Or you may be at the other extreme, closing yourself off to the potential of wonderful relationships because you are scared that opening your heart will make you vulnerable and subject to rejection. As ever, take the middle path, be open and independent, and your relationships will blossom.

Don't change only for the sake of your partner, or expect them to do the same. Just as it is very freeing to take yourself out of the box your ego has created for you during your life, don't be tempted to try and put others into boxes, or to label them. If you cannot allow others to be their true selves, how can you hope to be yourself? If you'd like to make a change, do it from the depths of your heart for you both; do it with a pure motivation rather than for a particular outcome, as there are no guarantees things will go according to plan—things will simply happen.

Listen to Each Other

Being a good listener is a practice that will nurture your compassion, cool your burning emotions and allow you to truly help others, in all your relationships, both personal and in daily life at work and meeting people. As in meditation, to listen attentively means to slow things down and set aside your own distractions and agendas. What is this person telling me? How can I be of help with my response?

LOOK INTO YOUR HEART

Think about whether you tend to see your relationships with others as profit and loss statements. Do you always mind whether people respect or admire you? And do you often feel that you are betrayed by friends out of jealousy? This is because you have forgotten something that has belonged to you since the beginning of time . . . your heart has the innate ability to smile.

Parents

One of the greatest lessons a parent teaches their child is respect. Because even without the wisdom of age and experience, respect creates a foundation on which to build compassion, kindness and love as your child grows and becomes their own person.

Many children, sadly, do not have a very good opportunity to develop a respect for the world around us. The food on their plate bears no resemblance to its natural source. So many are surrounded by concrete and manmade noise, rather than trees and the sounds of nature, and they just can't understand why it matters if they take care of the world or not, even down to the street where they live. Without a respect for their neighbors and what is on their doorstep, how can these children develop a respect for themselves? How can they access that natural optimism that is within us all? You might think it is a question of poverty and opportunity, but there are families and villages all over the world in which having little is no barrier to everyday happiness. Human beings need enough food to eat and a roof over their heads; without those, there is true suffering and, sadly, there is far too much of that in the world. But beyond food and shelter, material possessions play such a small part in what really matters.

While some children are not taught to have any confidence in themselves or hope in the world, at the other end of the spectrum, children are weighed down by so much pressure, they grow up fearful and anxious that however hard they try, they might just fail at being the best. There is so much competition now in life, from the moment a child even speaks their first word or takes their first step. By the time they go to school, many have already begun to develop a sense of self often based on comparisons with others, rather than on the seeds of truly understanding and accepting themselves. When we do see a child simply having a wonderful, free time taking part in something, without a care in the world as to whether they might be "the best" or not—how inspiring that is, so full of natural joy.

It's obvious when we see it, but in today's modern world, it often goes against everything we are taught: to have burning ambition, to be better than the Joneses, to earn a lot of money so that we may continue the cycle of consumption that the economies of the modern world rely so heavily upon. We have become so caught up in these cycles that we are passing them on to our children earlier and earlier. They know the difference between Nike and Adidas before they know where a carrot comes from.

The talents of children should be nurtured and encouraged, but if we become attached to those talents, our children will be too, and enjoyment may turn into fear. It is natural to want to praise our children; if we can do so without labeling them, then their hearts and minds will stay open and free. If we can accept our children just as they are, then think what amazing people they will be.

Turn Anger into Compassion

Holding on to anger is like grasping a hot coal with the intent of throwing it at someone else; you are the one getting burned.
• BUDDHA

If we don't have individual peace, how can we hope to have peace in this world? How can we develop this sense of peace and turn anger into compassion?

Peace is the natural state of your mind, of your nature. But as long as you struggle on under the control of your ego or your attachments, you will struggle to experience it. It is like a very poor person who has a great treasure hidden just beneath his bed, but he doesn't know the treasure is there. Suppose a smart person comes along and points out the treasure; he will realize he has this great wealth and will feel tremendous happiness and gratitude. Similarly, we have a great peace in our mind, but we don't realize it. That is why we struggle in our lives, why things become destructive.

There are things in life that just always seem to push our anger buttons. For some, it might be when they perceive a lack of common courtesy, like road rage or litter rage, for example. Anger may seem 100 percent justified, as in the face of a bully, or if a terrible harm has been done to a loved one. I think the key is to investigate our anger, rather than blindly follow it, and feel with our hearts whether it is an anger that is part of a healing process toward forgiveness, or if it does no one any good at all and just makes us feel very uncomfortable.

I think the frantic pace at which people lead their lives may often cause a sense of panic, so when obstacles come, which they always will, they are met with a rush of blood to the head rather than a calm, inquiring, "So what should I do here then?" And despite the advances in technology—which, on the surface, allow people to communicate with each other twenty-four hours a day if they like—we are experiencing fewer and fewer opportunities to connect with our fellow human beings. I feel there is much anger in the world that results from us no longer knowing quite how to communicate with one another anymore. It becomes as though we look at one another as complete strangers with nothing in common, even though we are all exactly the same. Rather than

connect, we tend toward making judgments based on very little,
or we are fearful of each other. We just don't "get" each other, and
in that chasm that grows between people, emotions like anger find
a happy hunting ground. We forget that we have the ability to inspire and lead by example and end up caught in fiery exchanges or
emotions that tend to get us nowhere.

Once we can recognize our anger, we can begin to think more
constructively around it, we can take a step to the side of it, breathe
slowly and deeply, and ask ourselves how we might better han-
dle the situation. It may even be as simple as saying exactly the
same thing, but calmly rather than with spite and heat.

THE "ANGER" BODY

The mind–body connection is never clearer than when a person is
consumed by anger. The physical manifestations of anger include
shortness of breath, a quickening pulse rate and often a feeling of
heat. But just as our body reveals the signs of anger, it can also help
us take the heat out of our feelings.

BREATHE THROUGH YOUR ANGER

When you are angry, you likely won't notice this in the moment,
but your breath is very shallow and weak. You may feel that you
lose the power in your voice even as you try to shout; it is hollow
and ineffective.

If you can feel anger begin to rise, then give yourself a chance
to cool the flames before they get going by focusing on your
breath. Breathe from your abdomen, slowly and with ease. Just

taking your mind off your anger for a split second may help take the heat out of the situation. Is it worth blowing up at this person or situation? Is there something else you could do instead, not to dismiss your anger, but perhaps turn it into a more useful action?

Anger Becomes a Habit

Anger is infectious and can easily become a habit you fall into, triggered in certain situations by memories and experiences, fueled by the ego and often by the world we live in. We see a person or an action, and it's like a match being lit; the same old feelings rise up. Perhaps you have grown up with a parent who is hotheaded and you follow their lead, getting into fiery debates over the smallest things. A part of you thinks that no one will ever listen unless you raise you voice. Or you're not quite sure where your sudden bursts of anger come from; usually you're a very calm and happy-go-lucky person, but when you see something that goes against your values, or you feel you are being criticized, all those peaceful feelings fly out the window, and you just can't help but blow your top. Have a think about it, and you will begin to see the patterns behind your anger. There may be triggers that put your vulnerable ego on the defensive, or certain things that you have very fixed and rigid beliefs about.

Don't battle with your anger, chastising yourself every time you let it surface. It's not something you want to bury deep inside, where it will literally eat away at you. Let it come, and give it time to cool down. When you are feeling good about things, spend some time exploring why you get angry, what your triggers and habits are. As you become more aware, you might find that little things that used to make you angry no longer have such a powerful effect on you. As you loosen your attachments, begin to let go of your ego and see the world around you with increased understanding and appreciation, you might find you can see things with a fresh view and be less hasty to react. You will approach problems with more creativity as you develop your inspirational mind, looking to finding a solution, rather than complaining.

Could you make a change in your life to help break the habit? Say you are filled with fury every time you see a teenager drop litter, but you feel powerless and even scared to say anything. Perhaps you might talk to others and find out a great way to inspire those teenagers rather than just shout at them. Reach past your judgment and find out if there is some small way you can make a difference. That is when you will show the greatest compassion.

As I said earlier, we often look for happiness in the wrong places, in what we *don't* have rather than what is already right here in our lives. In the same way, if you turn over anger, like a coin, you may often find compassion has been there all along. Parents and children might spend years living in anger with one another because of all their misunderstandings, when if only they knew to look, there is always something they have in common, a seed of understanding they could nurture.

So remember that anger is a great teacher. Sometimes it is telling you that you need to think through something to find a better way, using your inspirational and then your practical mind. Sometimes it is letting you know your ego is still quite firmly in control. Either way, listen to your anger, but don't let it control you. Your life is too precious for that.

Gossip and Harsh Words

While it is, understandably, extremely hard to practice compassion with people who physically harm us, we are also often hurt by words. Gossip is just wind, breath and air—hot air. But as ordinary human beings, we get angry or upset and want to get them back. Our habit is to react with negative feelings, words and even actions.

It is very easy to love pleasant people and situations. But the true test comes when you are faced with the most unpleasant situation or people, whether you can take it or not. Here, we can practice something on a day-to-day basis that really requires our attention. It is very important that we try to make an effort, and so, if someone says something negative about you, as an acknowledgment, reply by saying something good about them. If you can't quite manage to do that, just keep silent.

HOW ENEMIES BECOME TEACHERS

What if someone says something bad about you in front of a crowd of perhaps hundreds of people, maybe at an important party or event, something deliberately said to try to shame or embarrass you? Instead of getting angry or saying something bad in reply, realize that this person has offered you a great lesson. By making you angry, he has given you the opportunity to fight that anger. Because of this challenging situation, there is a possibility for you to develop patience, understanding and to sharpen your wisdom. Rather than regard this person as the enemy, therefore, look upon them as a teacher.

Do not speak—unless it improves on silence.

• BUDDHIST SAYING

If you practice love and compassion, then you will be able to stay calm and stay on your own path, even when those whom you have always protected and taken care of, without any reason, suddenly become nasty and start acting as though you are their enemy. This happens because of bad karma, not because of you. It is like a mushroom that springs up as if out of nowhere. It happens often and people can't understand why, so they become upset and angry.

These things happen because people are influenced by anger, influenced by jealousy, ignorance, ego and other nonsense. They are totally under the influence and don't even know it. Because they feel superior in some way, they may even beat or abuse you; they are blind.

However hard this may be, if you are the enlightened one, even just a beginner, then how can you meet hatred with hatred? Perhaps there is something you can understand about why they say these things. Otherwise, if we act like them, what is special about us? What have we learned?

Think too about how you might be tempted to criticize or gossip about others. Most of us are definitely fond of doing this. Whenever we talk about something or someone, within a few minutes we start to criticize. We can't help it; it's a habit. But who are we to really know this person—maybe he or she is even a great master in disguise. So it is always good to practice letting go of this habit we have of being critical of others. Because what other people do is none of our business. It's theirs, so let them do it. The best thing is to keep quiet.

In this way, we begin to speak more gently and quietly. With a pure and right motivation, you are bound to bring happiness. Kind words are important. And to make others peaceful, it helps to keep your own appearance peaceful. To do that, you must first be aware of yourself, because if your awareness is lacking, you might be able to keep a cool head once or twice, but one day you'll forget yourself. Awareness is important for everything; as obstacles pop up to challenge you along the way, you can knock them down with awareness. You can keep those burning emotions in check and stay balanced and on the middle path, rather than be constantly sidetracked and carried away. It isn't about being very rigid or conservative in life. Have a laugh, enjoy yourself; it's just that, with awareness, you won't need to have a laugh at the expense of others.

Compassionate Listening

A very good practice for preventing anger in the first place is to become masterful at listening. When we listen with true empathy, then we put ourselves in the other person's shoes and realize they are indeed a person, just like us. It is important to put judgment to one side when we listen; this is often very hard to begin with, as we grow up taught to judge everything we see and hear. But if we can simply be completely attentive to other people, then instead of anger rising up, we will seek to understand them, even if they speak or act in a seemingly very hurtful or unfair way.

Talk about your emotions and listen with compassion to others; understanding is a two-way street. If you can begin to listen openly and without any judgment to those close to you, even those who are most annoying to you, then you begin to see them with compassion. You can then quietly begin to explore your feelings around these people, turn them over like pebbles and take a really good look. Do you want to feel angry around that person, or do you want to stay peaceful and calm, no matter what they throw at you?

I hope that as you practice, you may find your anger cools as you tread with a lighter step. Nourish yourself with nature, with times of contemplation and reflection. Look for the things in life that inspire you rather than infuriate you. Talk to your friends, your teachers, and they will help you explore where it is your moments of anger come from and how you might do something about tackling the triggers that set them off. It isn't easy, but with less anger in life there opens up such a great space for inspiration, enjoyment and for simply getting on with the things that really matter.

Fearlessness in Troubled Times

Boldness be thy friend.
• WILLIAM SHAKESPEARE, *CYMBELINE*

We have a long and bumpy road to travel in life. I don't mind the bumps, but when I see the road stretched out ahead, that's a little scary for me. None of us knows how long the road is, and so we keep living on our hopes and fears. Like most, I enjoy the periods of hope, but, unfortunately, hope rarely comes without fear. Thinking about this spoils my breakfast. If you are lucky enough not to feel this way, then I wish I could take refuge in your boat.

For example, you have a great joy when you are about to have a beautiful girlfriend or a handsome boyfriend that you have been dreaming of, or you have just had that great promotion at work that you were hoping for. Sooner or later, these wonderful feelings will be accompanied by fears—that you might lose them, that things might go wrong, that you won't be good enough.

Fear and anxiety seem to be at epidemic levels in this modern age. If you live with high expectations of yourself and of life, then fear is natural, as you worry about what will happen if you don't meet those expectations or if life goes against your plans. And because life rarely goes according to plan, perhaps you have previously encountered disappointment, and you fear that if you take a chance, you will meet it again.

The trouble is that, when so much fear is involved, it tends to keep you stuck in one place rather than allowing yourself to go with the flow and just do your best. The best thing you can do is to look at your fears openly and honestly; don't dismiss them, but don't let them hold you back from giving life a go.

The ordinary or natural state of your life is really fearless, and if you tap into that natural state, it will give you a great deal of confidence. When you no longer feel the need to be perfect or compare yourself to others or take every bit of criticism into your heart, you can feel this relaxed fearlessness and confidence.

Imagine your day free from self-criticism or judgment of others, free from embarrassment or fear of "what might happen." Acceptance doesn't mean you don't care about the world around you, or that you shouldn't look hard to find your purpose, but it reminds us that we are none of us perfect, no better and no worse than everyone else. So why not go for it in life and be ourselves, rather than wasting time worrying.

Appreciation also encourages confidence, or fearlessness. As we realize all the things we have to be thankful for in our day, our whole attitude lightens up, becomes optimistic. If you can enjoy the moment, then you are more present, connecting with others, connecting with life. You come to the party, rather than staying on the outskirts. As you show your appreciation in others, that is a kind of generosity that will in turn bring you more feelings of contentment, calming your fears. If you can see the good in the world and people around you, you will see the good in yourself. Rather than be fearful of what might happen, you will be inspired to find out.

Being fearless doesn't mean you will never encounter fears, as they are a natural part of our hopes, which in turn are a natural part of life. Like anger, fear can be a great teacher. For example, when I am in England and someone asks a question, I often have trouble when listening. When people ask a question, they seem to first talk about what they think, and I am left not knowing what to say. I might feel confused, and so a little fearful in the moment because I am attaching my ego to the situation. "Is that a question?" I ask. That is just a tiny example of fear, but we experience these situations all the time, and so it's helpful to use our day-to-day lives as lessons.

For many, fear becomes extremely painful, even to the point of committing suicide. Sadly, these people cannot turn their fears into wisdom, as it has become overwhelming. The sense of "I" takes over, and the true essence of life shrinks beyond reach. That is why I say that acceptance is the highlight of my life. It is so freeing to know that you are OK as you are, that your best truly is good enough, to accept this in your heart. If I could pass on one thing, it would be acceptance. It is such a strength.

Preparing for the Worst

In Buddhist philosophy, there is a great deal of teaching about death and being prepared for it, because it is only by being prepared for our death that we can truly *live*. In the modern world, many people are so frightened of death that they hide away from thinking about it; to contemplate this one certainty we all have is thought to be negative or depressing. But I think the fact that people so adamantly shy away from death is the cause of more depression, fear and anxiety; whereas, if we are prepared, if we can accept that we may die tomorrow, then aren't we more likely to live and learn well today?

Perhaps it is the idea that, in contemplating death, we fear we may have regrets about our life, so we put it off, year after year. But by doing that, we put off our life, we drift along, or we cram our days with nonsense and put off our own happiness, when all along it is right here.

Or perhaps you find yourself planning your life away, always looking into the distance, running after future versions of yourself and your life, fearful of what will happen if you live in the now. You may feel that planning is the best form of preparation. It is true, of course, that you need to work hard so that you may have a roof over your head later on in life, but don't let that put you off living today. After all, making the most of today is doing the work you are meant to do to the very best of your abilities; it's about making the world a better place in whatever small way you can, not taking life for granted, and it's the best preparation for death you can have.

THINK ABOUT DEATH

It is a good idea to spend some time contemplating death when you are in a happy, relaxed state—when you've had a good day, so that the thoughts will not frighten you, but you'll be able to explore with an open heart and really have a good look around. These are especially good times for contemplation, rather than when our minds are clouded and filled with distractions or very difficult challenges.

The Fear of Failure, or Sometimes Success

When you think about beginning a new relationship or accepting a new job, moving to a new city or country, it's natural to have fears and uncertainties. You may worry you are making the "wrong" decision, or that you will somehow fail in this new path. At times in your life, this fear may become so strong that it paralyzes you and prevents you from even having a go, giving it a whirl to see what may happen.

Whatever course you decide upon, there is always someone to tell you that you are wrong. There are always difficulties arising which tempt you to believe that your critics are right.

• RALPH WALDO EMERSON

But if you are mindful about your decisions and choices in life, if you listen to and follow your heart, and then simply do your best, there is no such thing as failure. Even if that new relationship doesn't last and that person doesn't become your lifelong partner, think of all the lessons you learn through the experience. If you try something in business that doesn't work, then you take that lesson into your future decisions; it is a step along your journey.

I'm not suggesting it won't be upsetting if you feel things have gone wrong, but you won't be so attached to the idea that somehow you have failed. Were you nice and generous to that person, did you make that decision at work in all good faith? Then why blame yourself, why blame at all? If you can gradually remove blame from your thoughts, then fear begins to subside too, and frees you up to act, today.

Learn to stand up where one falls.
• TIBETAN PROVERB

You might worry that if you do succeed, then you will have increased responsibility and the stakes will be so much higher if things do eventually go wrong. I think this is a part of all the expectations that are loaded onto everyone's shoulders in the modern world. Some are expected to fail, which is so sad, and some are weighed down by so much pressure to succeed that they want to run away. There is the pressure to somehow do better than your parents did before you, better than your neighbors, your school friends. Many wonderful, talented people shy away from their true cause, their work in life, because of these pressures associated with success. They worry that the higher they climb, the bigger their fall.

This is why we so often talk about the middle path in the Buddhist philosophy. When you walk with balance, knowing that you are not too close to the edge, but equally you are keen to make your way, then you are not slowed down by these fears and so you will actually get much further. There is no need to rush to success or to fear it if you take things gently, step lightly, and make your decisions with a pure heart. Likewise, never be afraid of failure, because within a flash it becomes a very precious lesson, just like every single one of life's ups and downs.

When somebody asks me to do some kind of teaching or talk, I just do it. So, I guess I don't have that much attachment. I'm relaxed, so I just say whatever I want. If some people don't appreciate it, what to do? Or, if others do appreciate it, then, thank you! It doesn't matter. I just do it, say whatever comes—whatever spontaneously pops up. If I were very serious and rigid about it, I wouldn't be able to do it; I wouldn't have anything to say. I'd be lost without a list or some kind of chart. It would just become too difficult, both for me to speak and for you to listen.

The bottom line is to relax, to open oneself and be less formal. That way, the nonsense will fade away and you will feel what is right. You will just do it!

Our strongest tools for understanding and challenging our fears come back to love and compassion. Usually love is the one that goes out there into the world through our actions, and compassion sits inside and works away so that we can share love. As you develop compassion, there is less room for the ego and so less room for fear. This can take time, as often the ego is so strong. You have to first *accept* yourself, and then you will begin to have room for others too, and send out your love as radiance, perhaps first with your immediate family and then gradually to everybody. Nothing is stronger than love; it is the strongest power in this world and will keep you fearless.

Everyday Reminders

Compassion	Simplicity
Kindness	Reflection
Hope	Rejection
Fear	Freedom
Change	Time
Death	Attachment
Humility	Attention
Patience	Inspiration
Anger	Generosity
Tolerance	Control
Appreciation	Love

Come back to these words in your contemplation, whenever you are ready to learn about yourself and about the world. When you are feeling calm and good, you will be able to think and feel your way through even the most difficult concepts, being gentle, but also encouraging your thoughts and feelings to have a good exploration. When daily life has thrown you a challenge, if you can, take it as a lesson, and you will develop at an even greater pace. Remember the student who couldn't get angry?

Open up and listen to your heart—which word speaks to you today? Don't try to find all the answers in one sitting. Be kind to yourself and remember to look for the good; find out what you are already practicing quite well, and also the things that you would really like to improve, even a little.

According to Buddhist philosophy, there are a number of things difficult to attain in this world. Sometimes it is good to remind ourselves that we are beginners, and so these things won't just be instantaneous or easy, but are well worth practicing in our every-day lives.

- It is hard to conquer the passions, to suppress selfish desires.
- It is hard not to get into a passion when slighted.
- It is hard not to abuse one's authority.
- It is hard to be even-minded and simple-hearted in all one's dealings with others.
- It is hard to be thorough in learning and exhaustive in investigation.
- It is hard to subdue selfish pride.
- It is hard not to feel contempt toward the unlearned.
- It is hard not to express an opinion about others.
- It is hard to gain an insight into the nature of being and to practice the way.
- It is hard to be always the master of oneself.

Enjoy the Journey

- Spend a little time each day contemplating all the good things.
- Sometimes we need to remind ourselves that life is precious.
- Accept the ups and downs; don't put pressure on yourself to be positive all the time, come what may. If today was good, that's great; if not, it's OK.
- Remember that we are all in the same boat.

Your Everyday Body

- Think of all the incredible things your body does day to day. You walk, talk, take nourishment and energy from food; you see the world, listen to your friends; you are constantly feeling the world through touch.
- And what about all those invisible things: your heart beating faster as your loved one approaches, the warmth of caring human touch, the flow of happy endorphins as a thank-you from your body for that run or trip to the gym.
- Think of how stress affects your physical body, how your state of mind makes you feel. Likewise, how does your body feel when you are relaxed and calm? What are the signs of your contented body?
- Cultivate all your senses; look at the beauty in the world around you, smell it, listen attentively, remember the care of touch, savor each mouthful.

Everyday Happiness

- Every day we make choices and decisions. If you are ever at a crossroads, ask yourself, "What will bring me happiness, more than pleasure?"

- If you want to, you can bring harmony, happiness, understanding and enlightenment to the world. This can start today with simply sharing your warmth with others.
- Spend time thinking about what inspires you, what moves you. Seek it out in the everyday.
- Take just a little time to notice the details, the simple things. Make a delicious cup of tea for your companion in the morning, stop for a moment to listen to the birds, listen attentively at work, and find the thing you really want to say.
- Pass on a smile.
- Happiness will come when you bring happiness to others.

Take in the Scenery
- We all come from nature and are a part of nature; we are nature.
- Take the time to look around and enjoy the journey, and you will begin to get to know the world, yourself and what inspires you.
- If you respect nature, you will respect yourself.
- If you can slow down to connect with nature, you will find it easier to connect with others, letting go of your own agenda and anxieties.
- Allow nature to cultivate all your senses.

Walking Together
- Appreciate those people who give you warmth and support, who help to point you in the right direction. Value them from the depths of your heart.

- Good company increases compassion, loving kindness, wisdom and peace of mind. They embody the inspiring spirit of encouragement.
- Trust in your intuition when you are with people. What energy are they giving out? Are you a good match?
- Trust in the guru within, allow your natural confidence to blossom, and know that you can you be your own best friend.
- Keep a watch for negative companions, those who mislead us, or our own mental enemies that tell us we are not good enough, that stop us from stretching and growing.
- Nothing is impossible when we walk together.

One Step Leads to Another

- The past no longer is. The future has not yet come. So look deeply at life as it is.
- Are you spending time wisely? Are you relaxed and focused, completely in the flow of your task, or busy worrying about what happened yesterday or what may happen tomorrow?
- Today is the source of the future, so look after the present.
- Change really is good; it means that anything is possible, it makes the rhythm of life fascinating.
- Why try to control time? It's impossible. Much better to take things a little easier.

Step Lightly

- As the Buddha said, "Do not carry with you your mistakes. Do not carry your cares." At the end of the day, there is nothing you can take with you, so it is better to tread lightly rather than carry a heavy load of attachments and expectations.

- Let go of "I should . . ."
- Let go of attaching labels to everything and everyone. The more we can give freedom to others, the more free we will be ourselves.
- Keep an eye out for those "burning" emotions of anger, jealousy, pride, even desire. Don't let them cloud your mind and control your actions. Move them aside to create space for love and kindness, creativity and inspiration, patience and tolerance.
- Let go of always comparing yourself to others, and then you will be able to rejoice both in your own success and everyone else's.
- Give life a bit of give.

Slow Down

- When you slow down, you find so many ways to be connected with life—with other people, with your purpose, with yourself.
- Savor the moment and you will savor life; you will notice what truly catches your attention and inspires you.
- Mindful living makes life so much more relaxing and stretches out time so that we can do great things.
- When you slow down, you can stop to help others more often, rather than always being in a rush to get to your next destination.

- Focus on one thing at a time; enjoy one thing at a time.
- If you slow down and are mindful, you can ask your inner self any question you like, however difficult, and you will know the answer.

Develop Your Compassionate Mind

- Consider, decide and then act: that is the essence of training your mind so that you can get on with the life you really want to lead.
- With a little stillness, our thoughts become friendly.
- Begin by familiarizing yourself with the things around you, on your journey, in the stillness of your room.
- Contemplate your own ups and downs—how did your day go?
- Then begin to allow your mind to gently empty, to just relax. Don't try to "fix" it; it will repair itself, given space.
- Don't be frightened of the stillness and the quiet; it is like a cool, healing balm.

Everyday Love and Kindness

- If you can be happy in your own skin, you have the best foundation upon which to build love.
- Love is understanding.
- Kindness nurtures kindness; it is warming and nourishing to the soul. We can choose to be unkind to one another, or we can choose to encourage one another. It's up to us to decide.
- Love naturally makes us feel vulnerable, but how much

better to accept that the future is uncertain and go
ahead and take a chance.

Everyday Generosity

* Start small; it is more important to give unconditionally
  than to give a great deal.
* Don't ever force yourself to give. Find something you
  can give from the depths of your heart with joy.
* Give quietly; don't make a song and dance about it.
* Even if you can't give totally, give half.
* Give what you can, whether that is knowledge,
  protection or inspiration.
* Think each day of what you can do to help others, in
  whatever small way you are able. Practice
  mental kindness; be generous in your thoughts and
  words.

Everyday Patience

* Humility opens up your mind and heart to the lessons
  life has to offer you, while pride is always talking so it's
  hard to know what anyone else is saying.
* You don't have to be good at everything!
* If you can step back even for a moment when things
  get heated, then you will create a gap for patience, to
  see things differently and look for the solution rather
  than a problem.
* To have patience takes great courage, to be calm much
  strength. You become a very understanding person, a
  wonderful listener.

- Patience makes us strong in difficult times and humble in times of great success.

Everyday Discipline

- With joy in your heart, diligence and discipline take you far along your path.
- With inspiration and devotion we stick to our good commitments rather than saying we'll "start tomorrow."
- If you are looking to develop greater inner discipline over something like your eating or drinking habits, then rather than feel you are denying yourself, consider how lucky you will feel at the end of the day when you have eaten lots of natural, vital foods that give your body energy without weighing you down.
- Take it step by step, rather than trying to make one giant leap. Don't force it.
- Keep walking.

Dealing with Stress

- If you can accept yourself as you are, and begin to release your strong attachments and expectations, then stress too should lessen its stifling grip. If you can be flexible, you allow room for wonderful things to happen.
- Use meditation and contemplation to slow down your mind; think about what really matters in your life, and make a commitment to put those things first. Learn to sit still and your natural confidence will return to your side.
- Let go of winning and losing, of trying to be better than others. Do *your* best.

* Don't cling to your mistakes or criticism. Have the courage to accept them, learn and pick yourself up.

Relationships
* The freedom you give to others you give to yourself.
* Let go of doubts, and focus on the way a relationship nourishes and supports you; give it space, and it will help your own wisdom and compassion blossom.
* Gratitude within relationships gives them a warm glow. Ask yourself what your partner or friend really needs, putting your own needs aside. You will be rewarded with their smile, their happiness and, in turn, they will ask what it is you need.
* Be yourself, be independent, and also listen attentively so that you can put yourself in their shoes.
* Teach one another respect; it is the foundation upon which we all build compassion, kindness and love.

Anger
* Remember that peace is the natural state of your mind.
* If you can slow down, then in turn you will find your temper lengthens, and you are less quick to let anger bubble over.
* Investigate your anger; look beneath the superficial triggers and begin to understand where it comes from.
* Remember that basically people are all the same. Even if people speak or act in ignorance, we can remain true to our own nature; hate never dispels hate.
* Speak gently and quietly.

Fearlessness

- Fear is a natural companion to heavy expectations. Think more about what you are going to do today, and you will begin to worry less about what may or may not happen tomorrow.
- Listen to your fears; what are they telling you? Where there is fear, there is often something you care deeply about. Be gentle on yourself, but when you are afraid, it might be a very good time to act.
- If you can prepare for the worst, even be prepared for and accepting of death, then you have nothing left to fear. You are free.
- It is human to make mistakes; they are a part of life, so don't let them put you off.
- Be less formal, more spontaneous. Give things a go.
- Remember that love and inspiration will keep you fearless.

Enlightenment

Enlightenment means strength, and with this strength you are then able to benefit others. Most people feel that being enlightened means that they will become almost like a statue, sitting there, doing nothing and spacing out. Well, if you think that way, then you are not talking about being enlightened; you are talking about something similar to mundane retirement, which is very boring and very tiring to even think about.

Enlightenment is the final result of "perfect understanding," or development of perfect wisdom, perfect love and perfect compassion. The "heart of enlightenment" is also called *Bodhicitta*, which can be translated as "the heart of understanding," or "the heart full of understanding." Becoming a Buddha or attaining enlightenment means that you have become a Perfect Being who possesses Perfect Strength. It is not easy by any means to reach this perfection, but we can all walk along the path toward enlightenment, understanding bits and pieces here and there. Appreciate and rejoice, without any expectation. It doesn't matter if people are unkind to you, it doesn't matter if people betray you, it doesn't matter if people don't even say "thank you" to you; by appreciating everything around you, from happy experiences to sad, your life will become meaningful, full of understanding, joy, strength and fearlessness.

We can sit in the caves, hide in retreats and spend hours meditating—which is supposed to help in developing our understanding, or give us some knowledge about our experiences within ourselves and in our mind—but if we do not put this sort of understanding and knowledge into action, then all that we have learned and practiced is only empty words. We have to go out and help, little by little, every day, so that we will also be able to know how much strength we have. At the same time, this type of living will help us develop that strength. We will feel more relaxed about life, but with a stronger purpose too. We will have the confidence and acceptance to know ourselves and know that we are good enough. We will stop putting others and ourselves into boxes, giving us room to breathe and grow. We will be able to adapt to change, be flexible and easygoing. We will have the confidence to try our best. We will be free.

I don't have any special recommendation, but I just want to say, be there in your day-to-day life with some understanding. *Because* the path is there, a beautiful path, the practice will flourish. Human life is very precious, but it has to be cultivated. I encourage you to cultivate your natural energy and to constantly check yourself and investigate your thoughts. We are very stubborn and not easily influenced, but I think now is the time to do good. We can take our blinkers off; we are strong enough and I know there is enough love to go around. Be compassionate to yourself, even as you look at your mistakes and mishaps. Then, if others are less than perfect too, use your developing compassion to kill your anger and frustration. Practice this every minute. Life is the practice. As the Buddha said, "Now, everything is totally in your hands."

I sincerely hope this teaching will help everyone, including myself, to generate our compassion and loving kindness and make our life fruitful. The reason I talk and write and travel is for the sake of breaking down barriers between people and within ourselves. Love has no conditions; it is like sunrays shining on the earth. The sun shines on us all, but it's up to us whether we are open to the light, whether we want to open up our hearts.

I thank my good karma and all my gurus that my path is not a lonely one. Thank *you*, that's all I can say.

The road we are taking
is an uncommon journey that will last many lives.
Not many people are fortunate enough to discover this challenging path that will lead to ultimate happiness and freedom.
Meanwhile, my words are here to accompany you
while we walk together.

• THE GYALWANG DRUKPA

Permissions

About the Author

His Holiness the present Gyalwang Drukpa (www.drukpa.org) is the head of the Drukpa lineage of Buddhism, one of the main spiritual traditions of the Himalayas. Also known as the Dragon Order, the Drukpa lineage originated a thousand years ago in India and spread throughout the vast Himalayan regions. Drukpa retreat centers can now be found throughout Europe, Asia, and the Americas.

Teaching worldwide for over thirty years, His Holiness the Gyalwang Drukpa has numerous charitable projects that exemplify the core Drukpa message of service. His Holiness founded the international humanitarian organization Live to Love (www.live2love.org) to promote five efforts for modern compassion: environmental protection, relief aid, education, medical services, and heritage preservation. With active projects in each category, His Holiness was honored with the United Nation's Millennium Development Goals (MDG) Award in New York (September 2010), and the Green Hero Award, presented by the president of India Smt. Pratibha Patil, in New Delhi, India (December 20ll).

One of His Holiness' flagship projects is Druk White Lotus School in Ladakh, India. The school has received numerous accolades for sustainable design, including three World Architecture Awards (2002) and the Inspiring

Design Award from the British Council for School Environments (2009). An advocate of women's equality, His Holiness also established the Druk Gawa Khilwa Abbey outside of Kathmandu, Nepal, and in Shey, Ladakh, where nuns receive spiritual training and teachings historically reserved for monks. Known for their daily kung fu regiment, the nuns have been featured in an hour-length BBC documentary for exhibiting a new approach to female empowerment. The Drukpa lineage has the longest waiting list for nuns in the region. Known for the annual Drukpa *pad yatra* (Sanskrit: "spiritual foot journey"), His Holiness leads hundreds of people on "eco-journeys" each year. These treks last one to three months and cover hundreds of miles, where participants pick up plastic litter along the way to promote the message of environmental preservation. In 2010, inspired Drukpa participants organized a mass tree planting in the Himalayas that broke the Guinness World Record, successfully planting 50,033 trees within thirty-three minutes.

His Holiness will be donating 50 percent of all proceeds from the book received by the Drukpa Organization to charitable causes through Live to Love.